THE HAPPY LIFE BLUEPRINT:

A Holistic Guide to Personal Growth and Fulfilment

Dr Manju Appathurai

To my Dad who is my solid foundation

To God for holding my hand

Contents

This book is not just a manual, it is a journey of self-discovery. Trusting the process and following the steps outlined in the book will enable you to delve deep into your thoughts and feelings, and ultimately uncover what your ideal life looks like. By embarking on this journey, you will be able to identify your strengths, weaknesses, fears, and aspirations, and develop a plan to achieve your goals. The book is designed to guide you through this process, offering insights and tools to help you along the way. The journey may not be easy, but it will be worth it, as you take the necessary steps to live the life you've always dreamed of.

But first say this aloud:
I will only proceed to the next page if I commit to trusting this book and follow what it asks me to do till the last page.

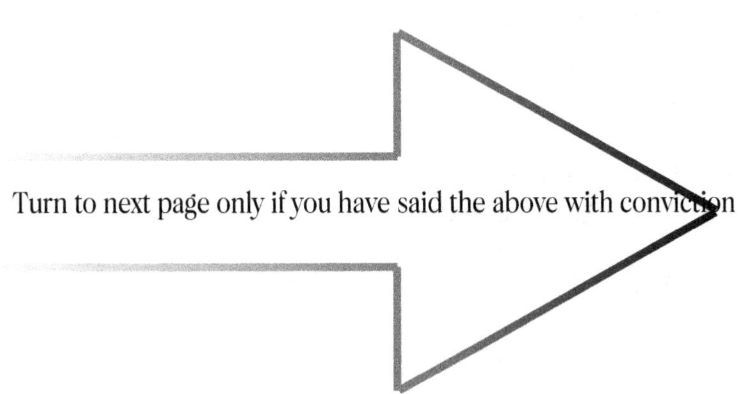

BOOK STRUCTURE:
How to Navigate this Book

This book is all about visualizing your whole life and setting goals and plans towards achieving that life.

However, some people have problem setting goals because they feel guilty and underserving or because they do not subscribe to visualization, or perhaps they may not know how to visualize. To ocercome this, I first explore what is stopping you or else we won't even be able to get out the gate. And, to help you along I provide two tools i.e. Gratitude Journalling as well as Visualization Techniques.

Next, we will get straight into planning our ideal life, by looking at 10 aspects of a hollistic life plan.

Throughout the book you will see 'My Story' because I want you to understand that I too was where you may be now, lost and confused. I felt stuck and didnt know how to move foward in life. I was overwhelmed. It is important for me to share my life with you in the hopes that it will motivate and inspire you towards your ideal life.

Also throughout this book you will see 'The Plan'. This is the actual work, the how to for everything I talk about, the guided asistance you need in implementing everything we will talk about in this book.

Now lets get to the book.

INTRODUCTION:
The Hollistic Approach To Life

Life is a journey full of challenges, and even the strongest among us can feel lost and unfulfilled at times. Depression and unhappiness are common struggles that many people face. However, it doesn't have to be that way. By taking a holistic approach to life planning, individuals can create a roadmap to a happier, more fulfilling future.

A holistic life plan considers all aspects of a person's life - physical, mental, emotional, and spiritual. It involves setting goals that align with a person's values, beliefs, and passions, and creating a plan to achieve those goals. The key is to approach life planning with intention and purpose, rather than letting life happen haphazardly.

As I write this introduction, I feel grateful for the opportunity to share my journey and insights with you. I hope this book will inspire and empower you to create a joyful and fulfilling life.

This unique book blends personal storytelling, practical advice, and scientific research to help you live your best life. It takes a holistic approach to life development, exploring multiple interconnected components of a fulfilling life: thoughts, emotions, personal character, spiritual self, physical wellness, social life, intellectual development, finances, career and love. By addressing each of these components, you can create a balanced and meaningful life.

Throughout the book, I share personal stories of my own journey of transformation because the most powerful lessons come from our own experiences. I emphasize the importance of self-awareness and self-compassion because personal growth can be challenging and sometimes painful. By cultivating self-awareness and self-compassion, we can make the journey easier and more rewarding. You will learn how to identify your strengths and weaknesses, set realistic goals, and treat yourself with kindness and understanding.

This book provides actionable steps and practical tools. Each chapter includes concrete steps and exercises that you can use to implement the concepts in your own life. Whether you want to improve your relationships, health, or finances, you will find practical guidance that you can apply immediately.

I have spent years studying personal development and worked with numerous clients to help them improve their lives. However, more than that, I have lived through many of the struggles that I write about. I have experienced childhood abandonment, the pain of heartbreak, the ups and downs of a career, depression, and suicidal thoughts. I know what it's like to feel lost and hopeless, but I also know what it takes to find hope and create a better life.

My childhood was a harrowing experience that left me with deep emotional wounds that took years to heal. Abandoned by my biological parents at a young age, I felt like a burden to everyone around me. Everywhere I turned, I saw happy families and loving parents, and it only served to remind me of what I didn't have. When I went to playgrounds, I would look at all the windows lit up in the apartments nearby and imagine happy families inside them. It was like a constant reminder that I didn't belong, and I struggled to find my place in the world.

My only solace was locking myself for hours in a cupboard where the world would disappear, and I could be anything I wanted. It was a place where I could escape from the harsh reality of the world and just be by myself. But even that was a temporary escape, and when I emerged from my hiding place, the pain of reality was still there, waiting for me.

Depression weighed heavily on me, I struggled with suicidal thoughts, and it felt like I was living on the edge of a cliff, one small push away from falling into the abyss of darkness. The weight of depression was crushing, and I didn't know how to shake it off. I resorted to cutting myself, hoping that the physical pain would somehow numb the emotional pain that I felt inside. But it only made things worse, and the scars served as a constant reminder of the pain I had endured.

Making friends was an impossible feat, and I genuinely believed that I looked like an alien, so much so that I would not allow myself to catch a reflection of me on any surface. I completely avoided mirrors. I was obese, and the constant taunting and bullying only added to my misery. It was like I was living in a nightmare that I couldn't escape from.

To make matters worse, I was cheated on in love and money, and I lost everything, even my shelter at one point. It felt like the world was conspiring against me, and there was no escape from the pain and suffering.

But I refused to give up. I knew that if I didn't act, nothing would ever change. So, I made the difficult decision to seek help and began therapy to work on my mental and emotional well-being. It was an uphill battle, and there were days when I didn't feel like I was making any progress at all. But I refused to give up.

As I delved deeper into the work, I discovered the power of self-love and self-care. For too long, I had neglected my own needs and wants, putting the needs of others before my own. But I realized that I needed to start prioritizing myself if I wanted to find true happiness. It was a difficult lesson to learn, but it was one that I had to embrace if I wanted to move forward.

Slowly, I began to realize that I had the power to change my life. I started to take small steps towards self-improvement, and over time, those steps became bigger and more significant. I began to prioritize my physical and mental health, started setting goals for myself, and actively worked towards achieving them.

In the midst of all this, I discovered the power of gratitude. It was hard to focus on the good things in my life when it seemed like everything was going wrong, but I forced myself to look for the silver lining in every situation. I started practicing gratitude every day, and it began to shift my perspective. Instead of seeing everything through a lens of despair, I began to see the world as a place full of possibilities and opportunities.

Finding my passion was another critical component of my journey. I had spent so long feeling lost and directionless, but I knew that I needed to find something that gave my life meaning and purpose. One day, as I was struggling with my own pain and doubts, I noticed something strange happening. Abused and neglected animals started showing up at my gate one after another as if it was a sign from God. At first, I didn't know what to do, but then I realized that taking care of these innocent creatures was something I could do to bring meaning and purpose into my life. I started rescuing them, caring for them, and nursing them back to health. It was hard work, but it gave me a sense of fulfilment and joy I had never experienced before.

I decided to turn my passion into something more significant, and I started my own animal rescue shelter. Over the years, we have rescued over 300 severely abused animals, giving them a second chance at life. Seeing these creatures, once on the brink of death, thrive and flourish brought me immense joy and reminded me of the resilience of life.

Today, I am living proof that it is possible to overcome even the most challenging obstacles and create a life of joy and fulfilment. The journey was not easy, but it was worth it. And now, I want to share the lessons that I have learned with others who may be struggling on their own journey of personal growth and development.

No matter where you are on your journey, I believe that this book has something to offer you. Whether you are struggling with depression, looking to improve your relationships, or simply seeking to live a more fulfilling life, the ideas and strategies in this book can help guide you towards a brighter future.

I wrote this book to offer a message of hope and optimism. Life can be difficult and overwhelming, but we all have the capacity for growth and transformation, no matter how difficult our circumstances.

This book is not a quick fix or a magic solution – it is a roadmap for a lifelong journey of growth and fulfilment.

So, I invite you to join me on this journey of self-discovery and growth. Together, we can create a life that is truly worth living.

What's Stopping You?

Before we go anywhere in this book, let's talk about why some folks have trouble setting goals for themselves. I'll tell you right off the bat, I've seen two main things that get in the way: a lack of faith and the pesky concept of karma.

Now, when I say a lack of faith, I don't mean they're not religious or anything like that. I mean they don't have faith in themselves, or in the idea that they can actually achieve what they set out to do. It's the classic case of "what's the point?" or "it's impossible, so why bother?" They just can't seem to wrap their heads around the idea that with a little bit of hard work and determination, they could actually make something happen.

And then there's karma. Now, I know some of you might be thinking, "wait, what does karma have to do with setting goals?" Well, let me tell you. Sometimes, people feel like they don't deserve to be happy or successful because of things they've done in the past. Maybe they screwed up big time, or hurt someone they cared about, and they can't seem to shake the feeling that they're being punished for it. Or maybe something bad happened to them, and they just can't let go of the idea that they're somehow cursed or unlucky.

But here's the thing: both of these obstacles are entirely in your head. You can choose to believe that you're capable of achieving great things, and that you deserve happiness and success. And you can also choose to let go of the past, and focus on creating a better future for yourself.

Now, I'm not saying it's easy. It takes time and effort to build up that faith in yourself, and to let go of those old patterns of thinking. But it's worth it. Because when you finally do set that goal, and start working towards it with all your might, you'll be amazed at what you're capable of.

So, to sum up, don't let a lack of self-confidence or the weight of karma hold you back from setting and achieving your goals. Believe in yourself, and believe that you're capable of great things. Remember, to move forward, we must leave the past behind.

Part 1: Faith

What defines our individuality? Is it our physical bodies? Our thoughts? Our emotions? According to some, the traditional concept of individuality is an illusion. In a state of ultimate realization, there is no duality of "mine" and "yours". We are all connected, and the inner self merges with the Supreme Self. It may sound like some trippy, hippy-dippy nonsense, but bear with me.

Once we reach this state of awareness, all problems and pain vanish. No more suffering, no more rebirth, no more death. We exist in eternal happiness and joy. And when our physical bodies dissolve, our consciousness merges with the Divine Self.

The consciousness of the realized ones is so pure that they perceive the vibration of the Self as light and sound. It's a life-changing experience that frees them from identifying with their bodies, minds, senses, emotions, qualities, worldly positions, or professions. Their inner bliss is unshakable, and the chains of karma dissolve. All attachments vanish.

The Universe is no longer outside of them, but something they embody. They become one with the earth, their consciousness expands in all four directions, and their energy flows through every atom of the Universe. They are the infinite space, and their consciousness encompasses the entire Cosmos.

This state of awareness is attainable for all of us. We just need to let go of our preconceived notions of individuality and embrace our connection to everything and everyone around us. It takes time, dedication, and a willingness to let go of our egos and attachments.

One of the first steps is recognizing that our bodies and minds are just temporary vessels for our consciousness. We are eternal beings connected to the Cosmos in a way that defies traditional understanding.

But how do we get there? It's not like we can just flip a switch and suddenly be one with the Universe. It takes time, dedication, and a willingness to let go of our egos and attachments.

Meditation and self-reflection are important tools on this journey towards realization. By quieting our minds and turning inward, we can peel away the layers of our ego and tap into our true nature. It's not an easy process, but the rewards are immeasurable.

Another key component is letting go of our attachments. We often cling to our possessions, relationships, and beliefs as if they define us. But in reality, they are just distractions from our true nature. By releasing these attachments, we can open ourselves up to the infinite possibilities of the Universe.

This journey is not about abandoning our physical lives or denying the value of individual experiences. It's about recognizing the interconnectedness of everything and finding a deeper sense of purpose and meaning in our lives.

As we continue on this path towards realization, we will encounter challenges and setbacks. But by remaining dedicated to our journey and embracing the guidance of those who have already reached this state, we can overcome any obstacle and attain true inner peace and happiness.

Part 2: Karma

Karma. What a mysterious and complex thing it is. However, I've come to realize that it's not as complex as it seems. It's merely a form of energy controlled by the information it receives, much like software. And, just like any software, the input determines the output. If I want to be the person I aspire to be and live the life I desire, I need to be mindful of the information I consume.

From birth, our experiences shape who we are today. Our family, home, friends, and choices - they all play a role in influencing us. Karma encompasses not only the consequences of our actions but also the memories that remain with us, affecting our future behavior. Although karma can be a useful teacher, it can also become a trap. If we cling to our memories and sense of doership, we can get caught up in negative karma, leaving us trapped in our past actions and bound to our bodies.

To break free from this cycle, we must detach ourselves from our memories and let go of our belief in our own doership. It's not an easy feat, but it's achievable. By adopting intelligent action and unemotional response, we can become aware of our actions and their consequences without becoming too attached to them. We need to learn to let go of our sense of doership and recognize that everything is happening according to a greater plan.

By trusting in the greater purpose guiding us, we can become truly free and start living in the present moment, free from the burden of past actions and future expectations. So, the next time you find yourself caught up in a cycle of negative karma, remember that you are not the doer. Something greater than yourself is guiding you towards a greater purpose.

Trust in this greater purpose, and start living the life you want - one full of endless possibilities for the future.

TOOL 1:
Gratitude Journalling

Why Gratitude

So now that we understand what is stopping us, let me provide you with 2 basic tools i.e. Journalling and Visualization Lets begin with gratitude journaling.

Gratitude is the act of expressing appreciation or thankfulness for the positive aspects of life. When someone is unhappy or stuck in life, it can be easy to focus on what is wrong or lacking. However, practicing gratitude can be a helpful tool in shifting one's perspective and cultivating a more positive mindset.

Research has shown that regularly practicing gratitude can have numerous benefits for mental health and well-being. For example, it can improve mood, increase feelings of happiness and satisfaction, reduce symptoms of depression and anxiety, and improve sleep quality. Additionally, gratitude has been linked to increased resilience, better stress management, and stronger social connections.

One reason why gratitude is so helpful is that it encourages individuals to focus on the positive aspects of their life, rather than dwelling on the negative. This shift in focus can help to reframe negative situations or experiences in a more positive light, leading to a more optimistic and hopeful outlook. Additionally, practicing gratitude can help individuals to cultivate a sense of abundance and contentment, rather than constantly striving for more.

There are many ways to practice gratitude, such as keeping a gratitude journal, regularly expressing gratitude to others, or simply taking a few moments each day to reflect on the things one is thankful for. By incorporating gratitude into their daily routine, individuals who are feeling unhappy or stuck in life can begin to shift their mindset and experience the many benefits of this powerful practice.

Gratitude is a universal concept that is valued across generations. However, the ways in which different generations express and experience gratitude may vary.

Now that we've covered why gratitude is so darn helpful, let's talk about what it means to different generations. From Baby Boomers to Generation Alpha, each generation has its own unique perspective on gratitude.

Gratitude Across Generations

For Baby Boomers, gratitude is often tied to a sense of obligation. Many Boomers grew up during a time of economic hardship and instability, and were taught to be grateful for what they had. This often translated into a sense of duty to give back to their communities and help those less fortunate. For many Boomers, gratitude is about recognizing the sacrifices of previous generations and passing on a legacy of generosity and kindness.

For Generation X, gratitude often takes a more personal tone. Many Xers came of age during a time of economic prosperity, but also witnessed rapid social change and cultural upheaval. As a result, they tend to value individualism and self-expression. For many Xers, gratitude is about recognizing the people and experiences that have shaped their own personal journey. They may be less concerned with traditional expressions of gratitude (like sending thank-you notes), and more focused on cultivating an inner sense of gratitude and contentment.

For Millennials, gratitude is often tied to a sense of social responsibility. This generation came of age during a time of global upheaval, with issues like climate change, income inequality, and political polarization looming large. As a result, many Millennials see gratitude as a way to promote social justice and make a positive impact in the world. They may be more likely to express gratitude through activism, volunteering, or supporting causes they believe in.

And finally, for Generation Alpha (those born after 2010), gratitude is still a work in progress. This generation is just starting to develop their own sense of identity and values, and gratitude is becoming an increasingly important part of their upbringing. With the rise of technology and social media, many members of this generation are growing up in a world of instant gratification and constant stimulation. As a result, it can be difficult for them to appreciate the simple things in life and develop a sense of gratitude. However, many parents and educators are emphasizing the importance of gratitude and encouraging children to express thanks for the things they have. By teaching gratitude from a young age, this generation has the potential to develop a strong sense of appreciation and empathy, which can benefit them throughout their lives.

Gratitude Across Cultures

Gratitude is a beautiful and universal concept that transcends cultural boundaries. It reminds us to appreciate and cherish the things we have in our lives, and to acknowledge the contributions of others. Across the world, gratitude is expressed and practiced in different ways. Let's take a closer look at some of these practices:

In Japan, the act of "goshugi" is a beautiful tradition of showing appreciation for someone's kindness or hospitality by giving them a monetary gift. This tradition is often observed at weddings, funerals, or when visiting someone's home. Another practice in Japan is "mottain-ai," which encourages people to be mindful of not wasting resources and to appreciate what they have. The simple act of bowing is another way of expressing gratitude and respect in Japan. It is a gesture that is used in various situations, from greeting someone to expressing thanks. "Naikan" is a reflection practice that encourages individuals to focus on the positive contributions that others have made to their lives.

In India, gratitude is expressed through "pranama," a beautiful gesture of respect that involves bowing and placing the hands together in front of the chest. It is a way of showing gratitude towards teachers, parents, and spiritual figures. "Seva" is another practice in India that emphasizes the importance of serving others and giving back to the community. Saying "Namaste" is also a way of expressing gratitude and recognizing the divine spark within each person.

In Hawaii, gratitude is known as "mahalo." This word is used to express thanks, admiration, and respect for people, places, and things. The practice of "ho'oponopono" involves expressing gratitude and seeking forgiveness in relationships. It is a powerful practice that reminds us of the importance of healing and restoring balance in our personal and social lives.

In South Africa, the concept of "ubuntu" emphasizes the interconnectedness of all people and the importance of community. Expressing gratitude is seen as a way to strengthen those connections. Gift-giving is also a way of expressing gratitude and building social bonds, with gifts often given to show appreciation for the contributions of others.

In many Latin American countries, "fiestas de gracias" or "harvest festivals" are a time for giving thanks for the bounty of the earth. These celebrations are often accompanied by feasting, dancing, and music. "Compartir" is another practice in Latin America that involves sharing one's resources with others as a way of expressing gratitude and building community.

In Indigenous cultures around the world, gratitude practices are deeply rooted in spiritual beliefs. Native American culture has the "giveaway" ceremony, where a person gives away their possessions to show gratitude and generosity. Smudging is another practice that involves burning sage or other herbs to purify the air and create a sacred space, expressing gratitude and cleansing the spirit. The practice of "two-spirit" or "berdache" honors the diversity of gender and sexual identities in Indigenous cultures, expressing gratitude for the uniqueness of every individual.

In Western cultures, gratitude is often expressed through verbal communication. Saying "thank you" is a simple but powerful way to show appreciation for the people and things in our lives. Writing thank-you notes is another way of expressing gratitude and acknowledging the contributions of others. Volunteering and giving back to the community is also a way of expressing gratitude and showing appreciation for the opportunities and resources one has been given.

Overall, gratitude is a universal emotion that is valued across many different cultures. It can take many different forms, but its underlying message remains the same: a recognition and appreciation of the good things in life. By practicing gratitude, we can strengthen our connections with others, cultivate a sense of abundance and fulfilment in our lives, and help us find happiness in our lives.

THE PLAN:
Components of a Gratitude Journal

So, let's dive into the components of my gratitude journal and how they can help you feel happier.

What did I do well?

Starting your journal entry with a focus on your strengths and achievements is a great way to boost your mood. It's easy to get caught up in negative self-talk and focus on what we didn't do or what we could have done better. But when we take the time to acknowledge what we did well, we shift our attention to the positive and build our self-esteem.

For example, you might write something like, "Today I went for a walk and got some fresh air. It felt really good to take care of my body and clear my mind."

Discomfort / things I shouldn't have done

While it's important to focus on the positive, it's also important to acknowledge the challenges and mistakes that we face. Ignoring them won't make them go away, and it can actually make us feel worse in the long run. By writing about the things that didn't go well or the mistakes we made, we can process our emotions and learn from our experiences.

For example, you might write something like, "I got really angry with my partner today and said some hurtful things. I regret that and I know I need to work on my communication skills."

Emotions

This component is all about acknowledging and processing your emotions. It's easy to push our feelings aside and tell ourselves that we don't have time to deal with them. But the truth is, our emotions are a natural and important part of being human.

By writing about how we're feeling, we give ourselves permission to experience and process those emotions in a healthy way. This can help us to feel more centred and grounded.

For example, you might write something like, "Today I felt really anxious about the presentation I have to give next week. I know I need to prepare more, but it's hard to shake this feeling of dread."

Lessons learned

This component is all about reflecting on what we've learned from our experiences. It's easy to go through life on autopilot, but when we take the time to reflect on what we've learned, we can grow and improve.

For example, you might write something like, "I learned that I need to set better boundaries with my co-workers. I've been taking on too much work and it's been stressing me out. Going forward, I'm going to say no more often and prioritize my own needs."

How to be better tomorrow?

This component is all about setting goals and intentions for the future. It's easy to get stuck in a rut and feel like we're not making progress. But when we set small, achievable goals for ourselves, we can build momentum and start to feel more motivated.

For example, you might write something like, "Tomorrow, I'm going to wake up 15 minutes earlier so I can meditate before starting my day. I know that when I start my day with mindfulness, I feel purposeful.

TOOL 2:
Visualization

If you're having trouble visualizing your future, you're not alone. Many people struggle with the idea of creating a clear image of what they want to achieve. Soma say they lack the imagination to do so. Others may call crap on visualization, but I'm here to tell you that visualization is a powerful tool that can help you achieve your dreams.

I used to be a sceptic myself. I thought there was no way that simply picturing what I wanted could actually make it happen. But after a few personal experiences, I am now a total believer.

One of the first things I used visualization for was to improve my mornings. I used to wake up groggy and grumpy every day, dreading what lay ahead. But by practicing visualization before bed, I was able to imagine myself waking up feeling refreshed and energized. And you know what? It worked like magic! I started waking up with a newfound sense of energy and optimism.

Visualization also helped me with my chronic worrying. I used to worry about everything, even things that hadn't happened yet. But through visualization, I was able to calm my mind and focus on positive outcomes.

Now, I know what you're thinking. "That's just coincidence!" But it's more than just positive thinking. Visualization is about creating a clear image in your mind and truly believing that it can become a reality. When we focus our minds on a specific outcome, our subconscious starts working towards making it happen.

The benefits of visualization are not just limited to me. Some of the most successful people in the world swear by it. Athletes use visualization to improve their performance, CEOs use it to envision their company's success, and artists use it to tap into their creativity.

So, how can you start using visualization in your life? Find a quiet space where you won't be interrupted, and then start imagining a specific scenario or outcome that you want to achieve. Picture yourself in that situation and feel the emotions that come with it – joy, excitement, confidence. Repeat this practice regularly and watch as your subconscious starts working towards making that vision a reality.

But remember, visualization alone isn't enough. It's important to act towards your goals as well. Visualization is simply a tool to help you focus your mind and give you the confidence to act. You still have to put in the work to achieve your dreams.

So, visualization is a powerful tool that can help us achieve the life we want. By creating a clear image in our minds and truly believing in its potential, we can program our brains to achieve our goals. So why not give it a try? You might just be surprised at what you can accomplish. But, most importantly, support it with a holistic plan, which is what the rest of this book is about.

THE PLAN:
How to Create a Vision?

Now that we've addressed why you are afraid to visualize, and we've explored your though process, let's get visual!

When it comes to achieving our goals and creating the life of our dreams, visualization can be a powerful tool. By visualizing our desired outcome, we can clarify our goals, develop a deeper sense of purpose, and even attract the people and resources we need to make our dreams a reality. But how do we actually do it? For those who have problem visualizing, try these ideas as we progress though the book. Alternatively, you may use any method that helps even just a simple pen-paper-list style.

Create A Physical Representation: A physical representation of your end goal can be a powerful reminder of what you're working towards. For example, if your end goal is to become a successful entrepreneur, you could create a vision board that includes images of successful entrepreneurs, a business card with your name and title as CEO, or a replica of a successful product you want to launch. Seeing these physical reminders can help you stay focused and motivated, especially during challenging times.

Visualize Yourself in The Future: Visualization is a powerful tool for achieving your goals. Take some time each day to close your eyes and imagine yourself in the future, having achieved your end goal. For example, if your end goal is to become a professional athlete, imagine yourself standing on the podium with a gold medal around your neck, or scoring the winning goal in a championship game. Visualizing your success can help you stay focused on your end goal and provide the motivation you need to keep pushing forward.

Use Music: Music can be a powerful motivator and can help you stay focused on your end goal. Choose a song that represents your end goal and listen to it regularly. For example, if your end goal is to become a successful writer, you could listen to music that inspires you to be creative, such as classical music or instrumental music. The lyrics and melody of the song can help you stay focused on your end goal and inspire you to keep moving forward.

Record A Guided Visualization: Guided visualization is a powerful tool for achieving your goals. It involves imagining yourself achieving your end goal in great detail. To create a guided visualization, record yourself talking through the steps you need to take to achieve your goal. Include sensory details like sights, sounds, and smells to make the visualization more vivid. For example, if your goal is to run a marathon, you might describe the feeling of your feet hitting the pavement, the sound of your breathing, and the taste of your sweat. Listen to the recording regularly to reinforce the visualization and keep your goal in mind.

Draw A Cartoon Strip: Creating a cartoon strip can be a fun and creative way to visualize your end goal. Start by drawing yourself in the first panel, then draw subsequent panels depicting the steps you need to take to achieve your goal. Include any obstacles you might encounter and how you plan to overcome them. For example, if your goal is to write a novel, you might draw panels showing yourself brainstorming, outlining, and writing. The cartoon strip can help you visualize the steps you need to take and the progress you've made towards your goal.

Make A Diorama: A diorama is a three-dimensional model of your end goal. It can be a fun and creative way to bring your goal to life. Start by selecting the materials you'll need, such as miniature figures, props, and a base. For example, if your goal is to open a coffee shop, you might create a diorama showing the interior of the shop with tables, chairs, and a counter. The diorama can help you visualize your goal more concretely and inspire you to act.

Write A Letter to Your Future Self: Writing a letter to your future self is a powerful way to visualize your end goal. Start by imagining yourself in the future, having achieved your goal. Write a letter to yourself describing what it feels like to have achieved your goal, including the emotions and sensations you're experiencing. Be as specific as possible, and include any advice or insights you've gained along the way. Seal the letter and open it once you've achieved your goal to remind yourself of why you started and how far you've come. Create A Vision Board: A vision board is a visual representation of your end goal that can help you stay focused and motivated.

Create A Vision Board: A vision board is a visual representation of your end goal that can help you stay focused and motivated. Create a vision board that includes images, quotes, and affirmations that remind you of your end goal. For example, if your end goal is to travel the world, you could include images of exotic destinations, quotes about the benefits of travel, and affirmations such as "I am adventurous and courageous." Place your vision board somewhere you can see it every day, such as on your desk or on the wall in your bedroom.

You Dont Have to be SMART

Have you ever heard of the SMART technique for setting goals? It stands for Specific, Measurable, Achievable, Relevant, and Time-bound. While these are great things to keep in mind, it can be overwhelming to ensure that every detail fit into these categories. Plus, who wants to spend all their time calculating and analysing instead of enjoying their life?

Instead of focusing on every single detail, start with broad measurements when visualizing your end goal for a happy life. For instance, instead of setting a specific weight loss goal, focus on feeling healthier and more energetic. Instead of setting a specific career goal, focus on finding work that makes you feel fulfilled and happy. By doing this, you can focus on the big picture and let the details fall into place as you move forward.

If you're feeling stuck on how to begin, let me give you some funny and inspiring examples. Let's say your end goal is to feel happier and more fulfilled in your personal life. Instead of setting specific goals like "go on three dates a month" or "spend more time with friends," try thinking about broad measurements like "have more fun" or "connect with people." This way, you can be more flexible and open to opportunities that come your way.

Similarly, if your end goal is to find a career that makes you feel fulfilled, focus on broad measurements like "find work that aligns with my values" or "feel excited to go to work each day." This way, you can focus on finding work that truly makes you happy, rather than just chasing after a specific title or salary.

Remember, the key to visualizing your end goal for a happy life is to focus on what truly matters to you. Don't get bogged down in the details and instead focus on the big picture. Life is too short to spend all your time calculating and analysing. So, go out there and start visualizing your best life!

And wherever the SMART technique may be needed, don't worry! This book will help you slowly build on it as we progress along.

STEP 1:
Your Thoughts

> *They cannot take away our self-respect if we do not give it to them.*
>
> *- Mahatma Gandhi*

When I first read this quote by Mahatma Gandhi, it really struck a chord with me. Growing up, I often felt like I was at the mercy of other people's opinions and judgments. I felt like I had to constantly prove myself and earn their approval, otherwise I was worthless. But as I've grown older and worked on my mental wellbeing, I've come to realize that my self-respect is something that can't be taken away from me unless I allow it.

It's a conscious choice to let someone else's words or actions affect me. It's a conscious choice to give them power over me. And in the same vein, it's a conscious choice to create emotional states that serve me, rather than ones that bring me down.

That's where Dandapani's teachings come in. By shifting my awareness to the part of my brain that I want to experience, I can consciously create emotional states that serve me. If I'm feeling anxious or overwhelmed, I can shift my focus to something positive, something that makes me feel grateful or happy. And in doing so, I take back control of my mental wellbeing.

It's not always easy, and there are certainly times when I still struggle with negative emotions and self-doubt. But I know that I have the power to choose how I respond to those feelings. I can let them consume me, or I can choose to focus on something positive and uplifting. And that's what mental wellbeing is all about: taking ownership of our emotions and choosing to create a positive, empowering internal narrative.

As I reflect on the power of thinking over the course of human history, I am reminded of the profound impact that different ideas have had on shaping our beliefs and perceptions. From the ancient Greek philosophers who believed that our thoughts shape our reality, to the contemporary authors of today who explore the complex interplay between our minds and the world around us, there has been a rich and varied history of ideas about the power of thought. Could all these people have been wrong from the beginning of history till today? Is there not some truth to it, maybe? Let me re-cap for those who have trouble believing in the power of thought.

In ancient Greece, Socrates taught that true knowledge came from within and that the mind was capable of discovering truth through questioning and self-examination. This idea laid the foundation for the power of introspection and self-awareness in later years.

In the 5th century BC, Confucius taught the importance of positive thinking and the role of thoughts in shaping one's destiny. He believed that individuals had the power to create their own future through their thoughts and actions.

Aristotle, a philosopher in the 4th century BC, believed that the mind was capable of reasoning and problem-solving. He emphasized the importance of logical thinking and critical analysis in making sound decisions.

In the 3rd century BC, the Stoics, a group of Greek philosophers, believed that individuals could attain inner peace and happiness by controlling their thoughts and emotions. They taught the importance of living in accordance with reason and the natural order of things.

In the 2nd century BC, the Taoists in China emphasized the power of the mind-body connection and the importance of aligning oneself with the natural flow of the universe. They believed that individuals could achieve harmony and balance through cultivating their inner energy and thoughts.

In the 1st century BC, the Roman philosopher Seneca taught the importance of cultivating a positive mindset and focusing on the present moment. He believed that individuals could find happiness by embracing the present and letting go of worry about the future or regret about the past.

In the 1st century, the Roman emperor Marcus Aurelius wrote extensively about the power of thoughts and the importance of controlling one's mind. He believed that individuals could find inner peace and tranquillity by embracing stoic philosophy and practicing self-reflection.

In the 2nd century, the Chinese philosopher Wang Bi taught the importance of mindfulness and the power of meditation in achieving mental clarity and inner peace. He believed that individuals could harness the power of thought by cultivating awareness and attention.

In the 3rd century, the Indian philosopher Patanjali wrote about the power of yoga and meditation in achieving self-realization and inner peace. He emphasized the importance of controlling one's thoughts and cultivating a state of inner calm.

In the 4th century, the philosopher Augustine wrote extensively about the power of faith and the role of thoughts in shaping one's beliefs and actions. He believed that individuals could find meaning and purpose in life through aligning their thoughts and actions with their faith.

In the 5th century, the philosopher Boethius wrote about the power of the mind in overcoming adversity and finding inner peace. He believed that individuals could cultivate a sense of inner calm and strength by focusing on their thoughts and emotions.

In the 6th century, the philosopher John Scotus Eriugena wrote about the power of the mind in transcending the limits of the physical world and achieving spiritual enlightenment. He believed that individuals could access a higher state of consciousness through the power of thought and contemplation.

In the 7th century, the Islamic philosopher Al-Farabi wrote about the importance of reason and critical thinking in achieving knowledge and understanding. He believed that individuals could harness the power of thought through the pursuit of truth and wisdom.

In the 8th century, the Buddhist monk Shantideva wrote about the power of compassion and the role of thoughts in shaping one's actions. He believed that individuals could cultivate a sense of inner peace and happiness by focusing on the needs of others and practicing kindness.

In the 9th century, the philosopher Al-Kindi wrote about the importance of logic and reasoning in shaping our thoughts. He believed that through the use of reason, one could achieve greater clarity and understanding of the world around them. This idea was further developed by other Islamic philosophers, such as Al-Farabi and Ibn Rushd, who emphasized the importance of reason and rational thought in the pursuit of knowledge.

In the 10th century, the Persian philosopher Avicenna wrote extensively about the power of the mind and the role of thought in shaping our perceptions of reality. He believed that our thoughts and beliefs could significantly impact our physical health and well-being, and that through the power of the mind, we could achieve greater levels of self-awareness and personal growth.

In the 11th century, the Indian philosopher and theologian Ramanuja wrote about the power of devotion and positive thinking in achieving spiritual enlightenment. He believed that by cultivating a sense of inner peace and devotion to a higher power, individuals could achieve a greater sense of purpose and meaning in life.

In the 12th century, the philosopher Peter Abelard wrote about the power of reason and critical thinking in shaping our beliefs and understanding of the world. He believed that through the use of reason and logic, we could achieve greater clarity and insight into complex issues and problems.

In the 13th century, the Italian philosopher Thomas Aquinas wrote extensively about the power of reason and faith in shaping our thoughts and beliefs. He believed that through the integration of reason and faith, individuals could achieve a greater sense of harmony and balance in their lives, and that our thoughts and beliefs should be grounded in a strong moral and ethical framework.

In the 14th century, the poet and philosopher Dante Alighieri wrote about the transformative power of love and the role of thoughts in shaping our emotional experiences. He believed that through the power of love, individuals could overcome even the most difficult challenges and achieve greater levels of personal growth and fulfilment.

In the 15th century, the philosopher and humanist Giovanni Pico della Mirandola wrote about the power of individual choice and the role of thoughts in shaping our destiny. He believed that through the power of human agency and free will, individuals could shape their own lives and achieve their highest potential.

In the 16th century, the philosopher René Descartes wrote about the power of reason and scepticism in shaping our beliefs and understanding of the world. He believed that through the use of reason and critical thinking, we could achieve greater clarity and understanding of complex issues and problems.

In the 17th century, the philosopher Baruch Spinoza wrote about the power of reason and the role of thoughts in shaping our emotional experiences. He believed that through the use of reason and logic, individuals could overcome negative emotions and achieve greater levels of inner peace and happiness.

In the 18th century, the philosopher Immanuel Kant wrote extensively about the power of reason and the role of thoughts in shaping our moral and ethical beliefs. He believed that through the use of reason and critical thinking, individuals could achieve a greater sense of moral responsibility and ethical awareness.

In the 19th century, the philosopher Friedrich Nietzsche wrote about the power of the individual will and the role of thoughts in shaping our values and beliefs. He believed that through the cultivation of a strong will and a sense of personal autonomy, individuals could achieve greater levels of personal growth and self-realization.

In the 20th century, the psychologist Abraham Maslow wrote about the power of self-actualization and the role of thoughts in shaping our personal growth and development. He believed that by striving towards self-actualization and pursuing our highest potential, individuals could achieve greater levels of fulfilment and happiness in life.

In the 1960s, the psychologist and author Norman Vincent Peale popularized the idea of positive thinking in his best-selling book, "The Power of Positive Thinking." Peale argued that our thoughts have the power to shape our reality, and that by cultivating a positive mindset, we can achieve greater success and happiness in life.

In the 21st century, the author and speaker Brené Brown has become a prominent voice on the power of thought and the importance of vulnerability. Her research has shown that individuals who have the courage to be vulnerable and embrace their imperfections are more likely to experience happiness and fulfilment in their lives. Brown has also emphasized the importance of self-compassion and recognizing that we are all worthy of love and belonging, regardless of our perceived flaws or failures.

The author and neuroscientist Dr. Joe Dispenza has explored the connection between our thoughts, emotions, and physical health. Dispenza argues that we have the power to rewire our brains and heal our bodies through the power of our minds.

This is further exemplified by the work of authors such as Eckhart Tolle, who wrote "The Power of Now" in 1997, and encourages readers to let go of their past and future worries, and focus on the present moment. Similarly, the concept of neuroplasticity has gained attention in recent years, highlighting the brain's ability to rewire itself based on our thoughts and experiences.

Overall, the idea that our thoughts have a powerful impact on our mental wellbeing and overall happiness has been present for centuries, with various philosophers, scientists, and authors exploring different facets of this concept. From the ancient Greeks to modern-day researchers, there is a consensus that we have the power to shape our thoughts and, in turn, shape our lives. By focusing on cultivating positive, empowering thoughts and beliefs, we can create a happier and more fulfilling existence for ourselves and those around us.

My Story

As I sit here, I can't help but acknowledge the incredible power of thoughts. Thoughts have the power to make or break us, to bring us up or to bring us down. It's a concept that I've struggled with throughout my life, especially during my darkest moments.

There were times when my mind felt like a prison, trapping me in a cycle of negative thoughts and self-doubt. I couldn't help but feel like I was drowning in my own mind, unable to escape the suffocating weight of my own thoughts. My self-depreciating thoughts were so debilitating I used to knock my head hard to stop the thoughts only to end up with a migraine instead.

From childhood I was always made to feel inadequate. It felt like no matter what I did, it was never enough to please those around me. The constant pressure to seek approval and validation from others consumed me, leaving me with a constant feeling of inadequacy. These thoughts only intensified when my depression set in. I became increasingly anxious and fearful of the future, constantly imagining worst-case scenarios in my head. This was my way of trying to protect myself from disappointment, but it only made things worse. I was always on high alert, constantly scanning my environment for potential threats, never allowing myself to relax or enjoy the moment. As a result, I was always so hard on myself, thinking that I had to be prepared for the worst at all times. This mindset made it hard for me to find joy in the little things, and I started to believe that any happiness I experienced would be fleeting and inevitably taken away from me. This belief became a self-fulfilling prophecy, and I found myself feeling stuck in a cycle of despair and hopelessness.

But as I began to explore the power of thought and the impact it can have on our lives, I started to realize that I had the power to change my own reality. I could choose to focus on the negative or I could shift my perspective and focus on the positive.

It wasn't easy, but I began to consciously shift my thoughts towards positivity and hope. I started to focus on the good in my life, the things I was grateful for, and the possibilities of a brighter future. It was like a switch had been flipped, and I was suddenly seeing the world in a whole new light.

I began to realize that the power of thought isn't just some abstract concept, but something that can be harnessed and used to our advantage. We can create our own realities through the power of our thoughts, and it's up to us to choose what kind of reality we want to create.

It's not always easy, and there are still times when negative thoughts creep in and threaten to bring me down. But I've with the help of many gurus' teachings, how to consciously shift my awareness to the part of my brain that I want to experience.

It's a journey, and there are still ups and downs, but I am grateful for the power of thought and the ways it has transformed my life. It's a reminder that even in our darkest moments, we have the power to create a brighter future for ourselves through the power of our thoughts.

The Plan:
Your Thoughts

Understanding your thoughts and conquering your fears is crucial for personal growth and development. It requires a willingness to dive deep into your own psyche and examine your beliefs, values, and experiences. It means acknowledging and accepting the negative thoughts and emotions that may arise and finding ways to transform them into positive ones.

Conquering your fears begins with identifying them and recognizing their hold on your life. Fear can be a powerful force that keeps you stuck in old patterns, limiting beliefs, and negative self-talk. By understanding your fears, you can start to confront and challenge them, gradually building the confidence and resilience needed to overcome them.

Understanding your thoughts, on the other hand, means recognizing how they impact your emotions and behaviours. Negative self-talk, self-doubt, and limiting beliefs can all hold you back from reaching your full potential. By becoming aware of these thought patterns and reframing them in a positive light, you can cultivate a more optimistic and empowered mindset.

1)   Life Lesson Learned

Creating a vision for ourselves involves a deep exploration of oneself, including past experiences and future aspirations. One way to start this journey is by reflecting on life lessons learned. By identifying the most emotional event in your life, be it happy, sad, angry, or disappointed, and what you learned from it, you can gain insight into your values, beliefs, and personal growth. These events can shape the way you view yourself and the world around you, leading to a more profound understanding of who you are and who you want to be. Below is a very simplified example but you should write with as much detail as possible and truly explore every emotion you felt. Detail out everything that you took away from the situation.

For each experience, do the following:

Date:
1 January 2022

Person(s) involved:
My husband

What I felt:
Betrayed, hurt, and abandoned

What happened:
My husband cheated on me and left me with no money, forcing me to fend for myself.

How did I respond:
I reacted by letting myself go, binging on food, and gaining weight?

What did I learn:
I learned that I needed to prioritize my own well-being and take care of myself, even in the midst of a difficult situation? I realized that my health and happiness were too important to neglect, and that I needed to take control of my life.

Do I want this to repeat?
No, I never want to experience that kind of betrayal and abandonment again.

What can I do to ensure this repeats / does not repeat?
I can prioritize my own self-care, set boundaries, and build a support system of people who will encourage and uplift me. I can also work on developing a stronger sense of self-worth and resilience, so that I can handle difficult situations with grace and strength.

2)   My Fears in life

Another essential aspect of crafting a personal vision is facing one's fears. By acknowledging and confronting your fears, you can move past their limitations and push themselves towards personal growth. This process can be challenging and uncomfortable, but it is crucial for achieving your goals and aspirations. By understanding your fears and taking steps to overcome them, you can create a clearer vision of who you want to be and what you want to accomplish.

For each fear, do the following:

My fear:
Expressing my feelings

Why do I have this fear?
*I have this fear because of my childhood experience of being
in an unstable family where I constantly tried to please everyone to maintain a sense of peace and stability. I grew up believing that expressing my feelings would only create conflict
and tension.*

How did it start?
*This fear started in my childhood, where I learned to suppress
my emotions and always put others' needs before my own.*
How is this fear holding me back?
*This fear is holding me back in many ways. It prevents me
from forming deeper connections with others, as I struggle
to express my true feelings and thoughts. It also affects my
self-esteem, as I feel that my opinions and feelings are not
valued or important.*

It this fear important enough for me to overcome it?
*Yes, this fear is important enough for me to overcome it. It is
essential for my personal growth and development, and for
building meaningful relationships with others.*

What one small step I can take to overcome it this year?
*One small step I can take is to read up on critical thinking
and how to express an argument/opinion. By teaching myself
to think and articulate better, I can gradually become more
confident in expressing my feelings. I will also start by saying
one thing to one person once a week at the office, gradually
building up my confidence and ability to express myself.*

Now that you understand your fears and have an idea of how to
change them, it's important to acknowledge that daily living is not
easy. Thoughts and fears will inevitably creep in and threaten to
derail your progress. At these moments, it's essential to have an
immediate coping strategy in place.

- Wrist-band snap: This technique involves snapping a rubber band worn around the wrist as a way to interrupt negative thoughts or emotions and bring the individual back to the present moment.

- Take three deep breaths: Taking three deep breaths is a simple yet effective technique for quickly reducing stress and anxiety. The deep breathing helps to calm the body and mind by increasing oxygen flow and slowing down the heart rate.

- Stretch or do a quick exercise: Stretching or doing a quick exercise can help release tension in the body and increase endorphins, which are the body's natural mood-boosters.

- Count to 10: Counting to 10 is a quick and easy technique for reducing stress and anxiety in the moment. It can help to refocus the mind and bring a sense of calmness to the situation.

- Repeat a calming phrase to yourself, such as "I am in control": This technique involves repeating a calming phrase or affirmation to yourself as a way to reframe negative thoughts and shift your mindset to a more positive one.

- Splash cold water on your face: Splashing cold water on your face is a simple and effective technique for reducing stress and anxiety. The shock of the cold water can help to wake up the senses and refocus the mind.

- Hold an ice cube in your hand: Similar to the wrist-band snap, holding an ice cube in your hand is a technique for interrupting negative thoughts or emotions and bringing the individual back to the present moment.

- Look out the window and focus on a calming object, such as a tree or the sky: This technique involves taking a break and looking out the window to focus on a calming object in nature. It can help to bring a sense of peace and tranquillity to the mind.

- Smell a calming scent, such as lavender or peppermint: Smelling a calming scent, such as lavender or peppermint, can help to reduce stress and anxiety by triggering the body's relaxation response.

- Listen to a calming song or sound: Listening to a calming song or sound can help to reduce stress and anxiety by creating a soothing environment for the mind and body.

- Do a quick visualization exercise, such as imagining yourself in a peaceful place: Visualization exercises involve imagining yourself in a peaceful or relaxing environment, such as a beach or forest, to help calm the mind and reduce stress and anxiety.

- Laugh, even if it's just for a few seconds, by watching a funny video or recalling a humorous memory: Laughter is a natural stress reliever and can help to reduce anxiety and tension in the body. Even just a few seconds of laughter can make a significant difference in how you feel.

If you need something longer when the emotion or thought is exceptionally strong, try these techniques.

- Mindful breathing: This involves focusing on your breath and paying attention to the sensations in your body as you inhale and exhale. You can do this for 10-30 minutes to calm your mind and reduce stress.

- Progressive muscle relaxation: This technique involves tensing and then relaxing each muscle group in your body, one at a time. It can help you release tension and reduce anxiety.

- Guided imagery: This involves visualizing a peaceful scene or situation in your mind. You can listen to a guided meditation or create your own imagery to help you relax.

- Journaling: Writing down your thoughts and feelings can be a therapeutic way to process your emotions and gain clarity.

- Drawing or colouring: Engaging in a creative activity like drawing or colouring can help you relax and focus your mind on something positive.

- Taking a walk-in nature: Being in nature has been shown to have a calming effect on the mind and body. Taking a walk in a park or forest can be a great way to reduce stress.

- Reading a book: Getting lost in a good book can help you take your mind off of your worries and relax.

- Taking a warm bath: Soaking in a warm bath can help you release tension in your muscles and promote relaxation.

- Having a cup of tea: Drinking a warm cup of tea can have a calming effect on the mind and body. Some teas, like chamomile or valerian root tea, are known for their relaxation properties.

- Exercising: Exercising is a great way to release pent-up emotions and improve your mood. Whether it's going for a run, doing yoga, or lifting weights, getting your body moving can help you feel better both physically and mentally.

- Schedule a time and place to express your emotions: Sometimes, we need to express our emotions in order to process them and move on. However, it's important to do this in a safe and healthy way. One way to do this is to schedule a time and place to safely express your emotions, you could choose crying in your room or screaming from hill away from crowd. This scheduling, knowing that your chance to express yourself is happening soon, has an effect of calming you down in the present.

But, regardless of all the advice given here, you have to find a way that works for you.

- All the plans in this book could take 1 to 3 days to complete but do not take longer than that.

- If you thoroughly embraced the plans here, you would be tired and some of you may feel overwhelmed. But remember your commitment to yourself and the book at the start of our journey

STEP 2:
Your Emotions

> *They cannot take away our self-respect if we do not give it to them. "If your emotional abilities aren't in hand, if you don't have self-awareness, if you are not able to manage your distressing emotions, if you can't have empathy and have effective relationships, then no matter how smart you are, you are not going to get very far.*
>
> *- Daniel Goleman*

When it comes to emotional wellbeing, one of the most important things I've learned is the power of choice. I can choose when to think, and what to think about. It's easy to get caught up in negative thought patterns, but I've realized that those thoughts only serve to bring me down. Instead, I strive to choose positive thoughts that uplift and inspire me. As Dhandapani said, "Water makes both weed and flower grow." Our thoughts have the power to create positive and negative outcomes in our lives. By choosing to focus on the good, we can manifest positive experiences and emotions. However, it's important to acknowledge negative feelings and experiences while shifting our focus towards the positive. It takes daily practice, but the impact on our emotional wellbeing is profound. Taking control of our thoughts and focusing on the positive can lead to a happier and more fulfilling life.

It's becoming increasingly evident that the state of mental well-being across the globe is deteriorating. With the rise of social media and constant technological connectivity, people are finding it harder than ever to disconnect and take a break from the stressors of everyday life. Additionally, economic and political instability in many parts of the world, natural disasters, and global pandemics have all contributed to the worsening of mental health. Another reason is the lack of social support and sense of community. This can lead to feelings of loneliness and depression, especially for those who are already struggling with mental health issues.

The world seems to be moving at an increasingly fast pace, leaving many feelings overwhelmed and struggling to keep up. The pressure to constantly achieve and succeed has only grown, leading to higher rates of burnout, anxiety, and depression.

The stigma surrounding mental illness also continues to persist in many cultures, preventing people from seeking help or talking about their struggles. It's a difficult reality to face, but it's important that we acknowledge the issue in order to work towards a solution. One contributing factor to this is the lack of education and awareness about mental health. Many individuals do not understand mental health issues, and this can lead to stigma and discrimination towards those who are struggling. More education and awareness can help to reduce the stigma and encourage individuals to seek help when needed.

The lack of sleep and poor quality of sleep is also a contributing factor. With the increasing use of technology and long work hours, individuals are not getting enough restful sleep. Lack of sleep can lead to a range of mental health issues, including depression, anxiety, and irritability.

Substance abuse and addiction can also contribute to worsening mental wellbeing. Individuals who struggle with addiction are at a higher risk of developing mental health issues such as depression and anxiety. Furthermore, substance abuse can make it challenging to manage existing mental health conditions.

Environmental factors also play a role in worsening mental wellbeing. Exposure to pollution, noise, and other environmental stressors can have a negative impact on mental health. Furthermore, climate change and natural disasters can contribute to increased stress and anxiety.

The increasing rates of violence and conflict around the world can also worsen mental health. Individuals who live in areas affected by violence and conflict are at a higher risk of developing mental health issues such as PTSD and depression. Traumatic events can have long-lasting effects on an individual's mental health, and without proper treatment, it can worsen over time.

Finally, the current COVID-19 pandemic has had a significant impact on mental wellbeing globally. The pandemic has caused many individuals to experience increased stress, anxiety, and depression, particularly due to the isolation and uncertainty it has brought.

Overall, these various factors contribute to the worsening of mental wellbeing globally. It is essential to address these issues and work towards providing access to mental health resources and support to help individuals maintain good mental health.

My Story

When I was just 13 years old, I felt so alone in the world. My biological parents had abandoned me almost at birth, leaving me feeling unloved and misunderstood. It was as if they had ripped away the very foundation of my existence. I couldn't understand why they would do this to me. Was I not enough? Was I not worthy of their love? In my teen years this feeling of inadequcy spiralled into a dark pit of despair, and it felt like there was no escape.

To make matters worse, I was constantly bullied at school for looking different. I didn't fit in with the other girls, and they made sure I knew it – I was called dark, fat and ugly. I felt like an alien, out of place in my own skin. I couldn't bear to catch a reflection of myself anywhere. I avoided mirrors like the plague, afraid of what I might see.

It wasn't long before these feelings of loneliness and worthlessness started to take their toll on me. I began to feel like there was no point in living, like nothing would ever get better. I felt so trapped, like I was suffocating under the weight of my own despair. And that's when I first felt suicidal.

I remember the day vividly. I was sitting alone in my room, feeling like I had nothing left to live for. It was as if the darkness had taken over, and there was no light left in the world. I felt so hopeless, so powerless, like I was never going to escape this endless cycle of pain and misery.

But even then, something inside of me refused to give up. Some small, stubborn part of me clung to the hope that things could get better, that there was a way out of the darkness. And so, even though I didn't know it at the time, I made a choice to keep fighting, to keep pushing forward.

It wasn't an easy road, and there were times when I stumbled and fell. But every time I picked myself back up, I grew stronger. I learned that I didn't have to be defined by the things that had happened to me. I could create my own story, one of resilience and hope.

Today, I am still on that journey. I still struggle at times, but I know that I am not alone. There are so many people out there who have felt the same pain, who have fought the same battles. And if my story can inspire even one person to keep fighting, to keep believing that things can get better, then it will have all been worth it.

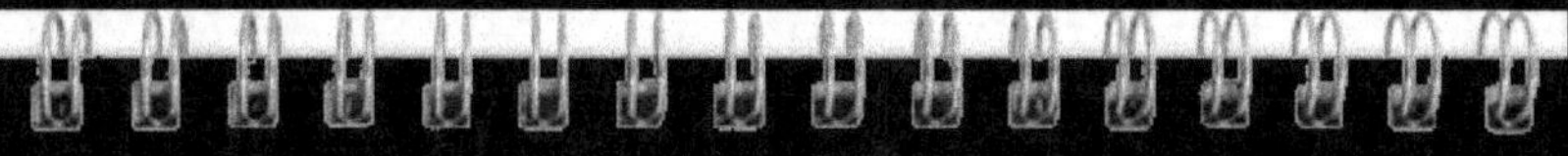

The Plan:
Your Emotions

Understanding our emotions is crucial to identifying the kind of person we want to become. By being aware of how we feel and what triggers certain emotions, we can make intentional choices that align with our values and goals.

List of all the things that makes me happy:
- *Spending time with loved ones*
- *Reading a good book*
- *Going for a hike in nature*
- *Listening to music*
- *Eating my favourite food*
- *Traveling to new places*
- *Learning a new skill or hobby*

For each, I will write what I feel and why it makes me happy:

- Spending time with loved ones - I feel a sense of connection and love. It makes me happy because I value my relationships with the people I care about.

- Reading a good book - I feel a sense of escape and intellectual stimulation. It makes me happy because I enjoy learning and exploring new ideas.

- Going for a hike in nature - I feel a sense of peace and wonder. It makes me happy because I appreciate the beauty of nature and find it calming.

- Listening to music - I feel a sense of joy and energy. It makes me happy because music has the ability to lift my mood and evoke emotions.

- Eating my favourite food - I feel a sense of pleasure and comfort. It makes me happy because I enjoy the taste and the experience of eating.

- Traveling to new places - I feel a sense of adventure and curiosity. It makes me happy because I enjoy exploring new cultures and experiencing new things.

- Learning a new skill or hobby - I feel a sense of growth and accomplishment. It makes me happy because I enjoy challenging myself and expanding my knowledge and abilities.

List of all the things that makes me unhappy:
- *Being in conflict with loved ones*
- *Feeling overwhelmed with tasks*
- *Being stuck in traffic*
- *Losing something important*
- *Feeling unappreciated*
- *Being in a noisy or chaotic environment*
- *Feeling trapped or stagnant in life*

For each, I will write what I feel and why it makes me unhappy:

- Being in conflict with loved ones - I feel a sense of sadness and frustration. It makes me unhappy because I value my relationships and want to maintain positive connections with the people I care about.

- Feeling overwhelmed with tasks - I feel a sense of stress and anxiety. It makes me unhappy because I want to feel productive and accomplished, but too much to do can feel daunting.

- Being stuck in traffic - I feel a sense of impatience and irritation. It makes me unhappy because I feel like my time is being wasted and I'm not in control of the situation.

- Losing something important - I feel a sense of loss and sadness. It makes me unhappy because the object may have sentimental or practical value to me.

- Feeling unappreciated - I feel a sense of hurt and frustration. It makes me unhappy because I want to feel valued and respected by others.

- Being in a noisy or chaotic environment - I feel a sense of discomfort and overwhelm. It makes me unhappy because I find it difficult to focus or relax in such environments.

- Feeling trapped or stagnant in life - I feel a sense of boredom and restlessness. It makes me unhappy because I want to feel a sense of purpose and growth in my life.

List of all the major negative emotions I feel:
Resentment

Analyse the emotions:
I feel angry and bitter towards people who have hurt me in the past, and I find it difficult to forgive them and move on.

What is the payoff for this bad behaviour?
The payoff is that I can justify not doing what I don't want / like to do and my bad performance – it's easier than actually gaining control over my emotions.

What price do I pay if I don't change these bad behaviours?
If I don't change my bad behaviour of holding onto resentment, I will continue to feel angry and bitter, which will negatively affect my relationships and overall well-being.

So, what can I do:

I can practice forgiveness and letting go of past resentments using the burn paper technique (this where you write down your emotion and burn it away and a sign of send-off). I can also work on assertiveness skills and expressing my needs and feelings in a constructive way.

Now I want you to assume you didn't do any of the things in this book, answer the following:

How will my life change?
Assuming I didn't do any of the things mentioned in this book, my life would likely remain stagnant and I would miss out on opportunities for personal growth and development.

What will I lose?
I would lose the chance to improve my relationships, my career prospects, and my overall sense of fulfilment.

How will I be happier?
Without acting towards my goals and aspirations, I would likely continue to feel unfulfilled and unhappy.

STEP 3:
Your Personal Character

> *Character is the result of two things: mental attitude and the way we spend our time.*
>
> *- Elbert Hubbard*

Character is a fascinating concept. It's intangible yet powerful - the sum of our habits, decisions, values, and beliefs. It's the foundation upon which we build our lives, and it's the lens through which others view us. But why is it so crucial? As Aristotle once said, "We are what we repeatedly do. Excellence, then, is not an act but a habit." Our habits shape our character, and our character shapes our destiny. To live a happy, fulfilling life, we must cultivate a positive character.

But what does that look like? Well, that's where the visualization part comes in. We need to have a clear idea in our minds of the kind of person we want to be and the kind of life we want to lead. This isn't just about setting goals or making plans; it's about creating a vision of our ideal selves and using that as a guide for our daily actions.

For me, that vision looks something like this: I want to be someone who is kind, honest, and compassionate. I want to be someone who is resilient and adaptable, who can roll with the punches and bounce back from adversity. I want to be someone who is curious and open-minded, who is always learning and growing. And above all, I want to be someone who lives a life of purpose, who makes a positive impact on the world around me.

Now, that's all well and good, but how do we actually cultivate those qualities in ourselves? Well, I believe it starts with small, daily actions. As the saying goes, "We are what we repeatedly do." If we want to be kind, we need to practice kindness every day, in big and small ways. If we want to be honest, we need to tell the truth even when it's hard. If we want to be resilient, we need to face our fears and challenges head-on, rather than avoiding them.

But here's the thing: cultivating character isn't just about doing the right thing; it's about doing the right thing for the right reasons. It's about acting from a place of genuine kindness, honesty, and compassion, rather than just going through the motions. It's about aligning our actions with our values and beliefs, rather than just doing what's expected of us.

That's why it's so important to take the time to reflect on our values and beliefs, to really understand what matters to us and why. This can be a challenging process, as it requires us to confront some uncomfortable truths about ourselves and the world around us. But it's also incredibly rewarding, as it allows us to live more authentically and purposefully.

Of course, none of us is perfect, and we will all make mistakes along the way. But that's okay; in fact, it's necessary. As the psychologist Carol Dweck has shown, having a growth mindset - the belief that we can learn and grow from our mistakes - is essential for cultivating resilience and developing a strong sense of self.

So, as we go through our days, let's keep that vision of our ideal selves in mind. Let's make small, daily choices that align with our values and beliefs. Let's be kind, honest, and compassionate, even when it's hard. And let's embrace our mistakes and challenges as opportunities for growth and learning.

Because ultimately, that's what will allow us to live a happy, fulfilling life. When we cultivate a strong, positive character, we become the kind of people who can weather any storm, who can find meaning and purpose in even the most difficult circumstances. We become the kind of people who inspire others and make a positive impact on the world around us. And in doing so, we create a legacy that will last long after we're gone. So let's embrace the challenge of cultivating character, with all its ups and downs, and let's see where it takes us.

My Story

Growing up, I always felt like I was walking on eggshells. My family was unstable, and I took it upon myself to keep everyone happy. I was the people pleaser, the comedian, and the one who could always diffuse a tense situation with a well-timed joke. But as much as I loved my family, my childhood didn't give me a solid foundation to build my own character on. I struggled to find my own voice and figure out where my boundaries lay. It felt like I was floating in a sea of expectations without any idea of who I really was. I was hollow inside that merely echoed what others wanted to hear.

It wasn't until much later in life, after years of stumbling around in the dark, that I finally started to find my footing. But let me tell you, it wasn't easy. When you spend your whole life trying to be what other people want you to be, it's hard to even know where to start when you're finally given the freedom to paint your own picture. But I took a deep breath, and I started to visualize the person I wanted to be.

It wasn't just about what I looked like, or what I did for a living. It was about my character. Who was I, at my core? What kind of person did I want to be? It was a daunting question, but I knew that if I wanted to live a fulfilling life, I needed to figure it out.

At first, I thought about the people I admired. What was it about them that made me look up to them? Was it their confidence? Their compassion? Their sense of humour? I started to make a mental list of the traits I wanted to embody, and then I started to think about how I could cultivate those traits in myself.

For example, I've always admired people who are compassionate. They seem to have a natural ability to put themselves in other people's shoes, and they genuinely care about another people's well-being. So, I started to look for opportunities to practice compassion in my own life. I started volunteering at a local charity, and I made a point to be more present for my friends and family when they were going through tough times.

Another trait I wanted to cultivate was confidence. I was tired of feeling like I was constantly apologizing for myself, or like I wasn't good enough. So, I started to take risks. I applied for jobs I didn't think I was qualified for, and I started speaking up more in meetings at work. It wasn't always easy, but the more I practiced, the more confident I felt.

Of course, there were setbacks along the way. There were times when I would revert back to old patterns of behaviour, or when I would feel like I was taking one step forward and two steps back. But I kept reminding myself that this was a process. Rome wasn't built in a day, and neither was my character.

And you know what? It's been worth it. The more I've focused on building my character, the more I've found myself becoming the person I always wanted to be. I'm more confident, more compassionate, and more authentic. And while I know that there's always room for improvement, I'm proud of the progress I've made. So, if you're feeling like you don't have a solid foundation to build your own character on, know that you're not alone. It's never too late to start visualizing the person you want to be, and taking steps to become that person. It might be scary at first, but I promise you, it's worth it. As Mahatma Gandhi once said, "Be the change you wish to see in the world." And it all starts with building your own character.

solid foundation to build your own character on, know that you're not alone. It's never too late to start visualizing the person you want to be, and taking steps to become that person. It might be scary at first, but I promise you, it's worth it. As Mahatma Gandhi once said, "Be the change you wish to see in the world." And it all starts with building your own character.

The Plan:
Your Personal Character

A holistic life plan is like a GPS system for your soul. Without it, you might feel lost and directionless, but with it, you can navigate your way towards a more fulfilling and joyful life. Let's start by creating a vision of who you want to be.

1) My nature
Identifying your nature is another crucial step in creating a holistic life plan. By listing both your good and bad habits, you can gain insight into your strengths and weaknesses. But here is the important step, I want you to examine how each good habit can be detrimental and how each bad habit can have positive effect on you. Understanding the opposites of your nature is essential in determining what type of person you truly are, want to become and what changes are needed to achieve that vision.

For each good and bad habit, do the following:

Good about me:
I care that I do not hurt feelings.

How this may be bad:
Caring too much about not hurting other people's feelings can sometimes lead to avoiding difficult conversations or situations that need to be addressed, which can be detrimental to your own personal growth and well-being.

Bad about me:
I assume the worst of the situation

How this may be good:
I can prepare for potential negative outcomes and take preventative measures. Once I've accounted for the worst possible scenario, then I can stop worrying and focus on the more positive possibilities.

2) What type of person do I admire?
It's also important to identify the type of person you admire when creating a vision for yourself. List all the traits that you admire in others, and use this list to gain a deeper understanding of the qualities that you value the most. These traits can serve as a guide for personal growth and development, allowing you to prioritize the qualities you want to cultivate within yourself.

Write also why it appeals to you and how the trait can benefit you.

For each trait you admire, do the following:

Trait I admire:
Staying calm and collected

Why it appeals to me:
I always get scared and want to run away. In the end, I don't get what I want.

How it would benefit me:
This would allow me to think better by not losing my head and make better decisions in situations where I feel scared or anxious. It would also help me to communicate more effectively with others, especially in high-pressure situations, and avoid saying or doing things that I might regret later. Overall, being calm and collected would improve my confidence, help me

to be more focused, and lead to better outcomes in both my
personal and professional life.

3) What kind of person do I want to become?
Finally, you can create a clear vision of who you want to become
by listing all the traits you aspire to have. For each trait, you can
identify three steps you can take to achieve it. One immediate
step, one within this year, and one more that will take a year or
more to complete. By breaking down your goals into manageable steps, you can create a roadmap for personal growth and
development. This will help you stay focused and motivated, as
you work towards becoming the best version of yourself.

For each trait you want for yourself, do the following:

Trait I want:
Self-discipline

Why I want it:
I often struggle with procrastination and lack of focus, and I
want to be able to consistently stick to my goals and priorities.

How it would benefit me:
Developing self-discipline would allow me to accomplish
more, improve my productivity and time management skills,
and ultimately lead to greater success and fulfilment in both
my personal and professional life.

Three steps to achieve self-discipline:

• Immediate step: Start small by setting a daily routine and
sticking to it. This could include setting a consistent wake-up
time, scheduling breaks and exercise, and creating a to-do
list for the day.

• Within this year: Practice delaying gratification by avoiding
distractions and staying focused on long-term goals. This

could involve setting up a reward system for accomplishing tasks, avoiding time-wasting activities, and regularly assessing progress towards goals.

• Within one year or more: Establish a long-term habit of self-discipline by creating a daily or weekly schedule that aligns with my goals, breaking down larger projects into manageable tasks, and consistently following through on commitments. This could involve seeking support and accountability from others, tracking progress towards goals, and adjusting the plan as needed.

STEP 4:
Your Spiritual Self

> *Most importantly, the meaning of spirituality lays the seeds for our destiny and the path we must follow.*
>
> *- Dennis Banks*

When it comes to finding happiness and fulfilment in life, there are a few key experiences that I have found to be crucial. One of these experiences is the feeling of oneness – that sense of connection with a higher power that fills me with peace and reassurance. For me, this higher power is God, but it could be something else for you. The important thing is to find that sense of oneness, that feeling of being a small part of something greater, because it can bring so much comfort and perspective to our lives.

Another experience that I have found to be incredibly important is the feeling of contribution. When I am able to contribute something positive to the world, whether it's through my work, my relationships, or my hobbies, I feel like I am fulfilling my higher purpose. This can be a powerful motivator for me, and it helps me to stay focused on what really matters in life.

Of course, becoming a better person is also a crucial part of the happiness journey. For me, this means working on self-actualization – becoming the best version of myself that I can be. This involves a lot of introspection, self-reflection, and personal growth, but it is so worth it in the end. When I am able to look back on my life and see how far I have come, it fills me with a sense of pride and accomplishment.

Perhaps one of the most important experiences for me, however, is the experience of inner peace. This is something that can be elusive at times, but when I am able to find it, it is truly transformative. Inner peace allows me to let go of stress, anxiety, and worry, and to simply be in the moment. It allows me to connect more deeply with myself and with others, and it brings a sense of calm and tranquillity to my life that is hard to find in any other way.

At the end of the day, however, it's not just about experiencing these things – it's about what I do with them. I've learned that I can't just wait for happiness and fulfilment to come to me – I have to actively seek them out and create them for myself. I have to become the cause of the effect I want, and that means acting, making changes, and putting in the work to create the life I truly want.

In all of these experiences – oneness, contribution, becoming a better person, and inner peace – there is a common thread: the idea that we are not alone in the world, and that we have the power to create positive change in our lives and in the world around us. It's a powerful and inspiring message, and one that I am grateful to have learned through my own experiences. I hope that by sharing my journey with you, I can help you to find your own path to happiness and fulfilment, and to experience these powerful and transformative moments for yourself.

My Story

I struggled for a long time to find a spiritual connection that felt genuine to me. I was looking for a way to hear God's voice, a guide to help me navigate through life's uncertainties. I tried everything I could think of, from meditation to mindfulness, but nothing seemed to work. I felt lost and alone, and life seemed to be unfair as the people who had been unkind to me seemed to get away with it, while I suffered the consequences. It took me a long time to realize that finding inner peace and quietness was the key to hearing God's voice.

However, finding inner peace and quietness wasn't easy for me. I tried different things, but nothing seemed to stick. I tried meditation, but my mind would wander, and I couldn't focus. I tried mindfulness, but I found it hard to stay present. I felt like I was failing at every turn. It was frustrating and disheartening.

But then, I started to find comfort in the little things. I would spend time staring at the clouds, watching them drift across the sky, and it brought me a sense of calm. I started to find emotional release in crying, allowing myself to feel my emotions and let them out. Playing with animals brought me a sense of joy and connection, and I started to see the beauty in the world around me.

It wasn't until I found a cause that I truly believed in, that things started to shift. I started my own animal rescue shelter, and it became a way for me to give back to the world, to make a difference in the lives of animals who had been abandoned or mistreated. It gave me a sense of purpose, and it helped me to connect with something greater than myself.

Through these experiences, I started to realize that the simple things in life were often the most meaningful. It wasn't about following a specific spiritual practice or adhering to a set of rules. It was about finding what worked for me, what brought me peace and joy, and what helped me to connect with the world around me.

In the end, it was these simple things that helped me to hear God's voice. It wasn't a booming voice from the heavens or a mystical experience. It was a quiet whisper, a sense of knowing that I was on the right path, and that God was with me every step of the way.

The Plan:
Your Spiritual Self

When I focus on the experience of oneness, I am reminded that I am not alone and that God is with me every step of the way. This brings a sense of comfort and strength to face any challenges that come my way. The experience of contribution gives me a sense of purpose and fulfilment as I work towards achieving my higher purpose. As I strive towards self-actualization, I am constantly becoming a better version of myself, growing and learning along the way. This journey towards personal growth and development leads to inner peace, which is invaluable. I am reminded that when I change my daily behaviour, I can change my life and experience the fullness of these experiences.

List of all my spiritual goals:
- *To attain inner peace.*

List of all my spiritual practice:
- *Practice kindness.*

STEP 5:
Your Physical Wellness

> *He who has health, has hope; and he who has hope, has everything..*
>
> *- Thomas Carlyle*

When it comes to health and wellness, it's all about having a strong enough purpose to keep you on track, rain or shine. You can't just say, "I don't know! I don't care! I can't help myself!" and expect to make progress. You have to dig deep and find the motivation to keep going, no matter what obstacles come your way.

Prioritizing your health leads to positive habits, creating a feedback loop of feeling better physically and mentally, which leads to even more motivation to continue healthy habits. Conversely, neglecting your health can lead to a negative feedback loop, where poor health habits lead to feeling worse physically and mentally, making it even harder to break unhealthy habits.

So, whether I'm hitting the gym, practicing mindfulness, or just making sure I'm getting enough sleep, I know that every little step I take towards better health and wellness is a step towards a happier, more fulfilling life. And when the rain comes pouring down, I'll be ready to weather the storm and come out even stronger on the other side.

Firstly, let's look at relationships. It's no secret that physical attraction plays a role in forming romantic relationships. And while looks aren't everything, taking care of your physical health can certainly improve your chances of finding a partner. Maintaining a healthy weight, having clear skin, and smelling fresh can make you more attractive to potential partners. Additionally, being in good physical health can help you have a more fulfilling sex life, leading to greater intimacy and connection with your partner.

Secondly, if you're in a relationship and it ends, it's natural to feel sad and disappointed. However, if you neglect your health and wellness during the relationship, the impact of the breakup can be even more severe. Not taking care of your body can lead to a weakened immune system, making you more vulnerable to illness and injury. This can exacerbate feelings of depression and anxiety, making it even harder to move on from the relationship.

Thirdly, social life is an important aspect of our overall well-being. When you prioritize your health, you're more likely to have the energy and confidence to engage in social activities. Whether it's going out with friends, joining a club, or attending a party, being in good physical health can help you feel more comfortable and present in social situations. Additionally, exercise and other physical activities can help alleviate stress and anxiety, making it easier to connect with others.

Fourthly, having good health and wellness can impact your career success. When you're in good physical shape, you're better able to handle the physical demands of your job, whether that means lifting heavy objects or being on your feet for long periods. Additionally, having good mental health can help you stay focused and productive at work, leading to better job performance and potentially more opportunities for advancement.

Fifthly, taking care of your health and wellness can help you maintain good relationships with friends, family, and colleagues. When you feel good about yourself, you're more likely to be kind and compassionate towards others. Additionally, when you're healthy, you're less likely to cancel plans or miss work due to illness or injury, which can help build trust and respect with those around you.

Sixthly, when you prioritize your health, you're more likely to engage in healthy habits and avoid unhealthy ones. This can lead to a positive feedback loop, where you feel better physically and mentally, leading to even more motivation to continue healthy habits. Conversely, neglecting your health can lead to a negative feedback loop, where poor health habits lead to feeling worse physically and mentally, making it even harder to break unhealthy habits.

Finally, good health and wellness can help you live a longer, more fulfilling life. When you're healthy, you're better able to enjoy all the activities and experiences that life has to offer, from traveling to trying new hobbies. Additionally, when you're healthy, you're more likely to have the energy and motivation to pursue your goals and dreams, leading to greater overall satisfaction with life.

My Story

Growing up, I always felt like I was different from my peers. While everyone else seemed to have it all together, I was always the overweight kid who struggled to keep up in gym class. My PE teacher made it clear that I was the weak link, and I'll never forget the humiliation of having the entire class come to my aid when I couldn't complete a somersault on my own. It was a defining moment for me, one that left me feeling utterly inadequate and unworthy.

As I got older, things only got worse. While my peers started to explore relationships and date boys, I felt completely invisible. I would watch as the pretty girls seemed to effortlessly attract attention from the opposite sex, while I remained firmly in the background, too self-conscious to even try. I couldn't help but feel jealous and resentful, and the more I dwelled on these negative emotions, the worse I felt about myself.

I turned to food as a way to cope with the pain of feeling so out of place in the world. Eating became a way to soothe my emotions and numb the constant feelings of loneliness and inadequacy. But with each pound I gained, my self-esteem plummeted even further. I felt like I was stuck in a cycle that I couldn't escape from – the more I ate, the worse I felt, and the worse I felt, the more I ate.

It took me years to realize that the only way out of this cycle was to take control of my health and wellness. I started by educating myself about fitness and nutrition, learning what worked for my body and what didn't. I also became more aware of my emotional eating patterns, and worked hard to counter them with healthier habits. It was a long and difficult journey. It wasn't easy, and there were times when I felt like giving up. But I knew that I had to keep pushing forward if I wanted to see real progress.

Through my journey, I've learned that healthy eating is just as important as exercise when it comes to achieving my goals. I've prioritized eating nutritious, whole foods to make sure my body gets the nutrients it needs to function at its best. And I've learned to recognize my emotional eating triggers and counter them with healthier habits, like going for a walk or calling a friend.

Now, I'm proud of the progress I've made. I may not be at my ideal body weight yet, but I know what works for me, and I know how to get there. More importantly, I've gained confidence and self-respect that I never thought was possible. I've learned that taking care of my body is not just about looking good, it's about feeling good too. And that feeling extends to my mental health as well. When I take care of my body, I feel more energized, focused, and positive. My mental health is stronger, and I'm better equipped to handle life's challenges.

Looking back, I'm grateful for the struggles I've faced. They've taught me resilience, determination, and self-love. They've given me the tools I need to take control of my life and make positive changes. And most importantly, they've shown me that it's never too late to start on a path to a healthier, happier life. If I can do it, so can anyone else.

The Plan:
Your Physical Wellness

What are my goals?
My goal is to lose weight and fit into my beautiful dress.

Where do I fail?
I tend to give into unhealthy eating habits and neglect regular exercise.

If I don't change this, how will it impact all other aspects of my life?

Thoughts:
I will feel negative and self-critical about my inability to make positive changes in my life. I may also feel helpless and discouraged about achieving my goals.

Emotions:
I will likely experience low self-esteem and may struggle with anxiety and depression.

Spiritually:
My relationship with my body may suffer, which can affect my overall sense of well-being and connection to myself and others.

Career:

My productivity and ability to focus may be affected, which can impact my performance and potentially my career advancement.

Intellectual: I may struggle with focus and productivity as my energy levels and mood are impacted by my unhealthy habits.

Social: I may avoid social situations or feel self-conscious in them due to my lack of confidence in my appearance.

Love:

My romantic relationships may be affected as I struggle with feeling attractive and confident in myself.

What is my action?

- *Immediate: I will start by cutting out sugary drinks and processed foods from my diet.*

- *Short-term: I will commit to exercising for at least 30 minutes a day, 5 days a week.*

- *Long-term: I will work towards a sustainable healthy lifestyle by meal planning and finding physical activities that I enjoy, such as hiking or yoga.*

STEP 6:
Your Social Life

The topic of friendship is close to my heart. Having great friends is one of the most important things in my life. They make me laugh, support me through tough times, and help me grow into a better person. To find and maintain these amazing relationships, it's important to understand that we become like the people we spend time with. That's why it's crucial to choose our friends carefully. I want friends who inspire me, challenge me, and help me become the best version of myself. So, I look for people who share my values and passions.

When we surround ourselves with positive and supportive people, it's easier to stay motivated and inspired to pursue our dreams. On the other hand, negative and toxic

friendships can drag us down and hold us back from achieving our goals. To ensure that we have the right kind of friends in our lives, we should get clear on our social values. What do we value in a friendship? Is it honesty, loyalty, support, humour, or something else? Once we have a clear idea of our values, we can seek out friends who share those values and are likely to be positive influences on our lives

Positivity is crucial when it comes to building great friendships. I avoid gossip and negative talk and instead focus on discussing new ideas and possibilities. It's so much more fun to talk about our dreams and goals than to complain about other people. By staying positive and focused on growth, we create an environment that's conducive to deepening our relationships.

Being the right friend is also important. I ask myself, "Am I the kind of friend that I want to have?" I listen actively and offer support when my friends need it. I try to stay in touch and show my appreciation. It's important to regularly check in with myself and make sure I'm being the kind of friend that I would want in my life.

I make sure to actively nurture my friendships. That means showing up for my friends when they need me and offering practical assistance whenever possible. Whether it's helping them move apartments or offering a listening ear during a tough time, I do my best to be there for my friends. I also make time to meet up regularly and have fun together. Friendship is supposed to be enjoyable!

Of course, friendships require effort and commitment from both sides. You should mutually be offering practical assistance when needed and being there to listen and provide emotional support. By actively pursuing our own goals and inspiring our friends to do the same, we can build a strong and meaningful network of friends who move and grow us in all the right ways.

However, it's equally important to let go of any anchors in your life that hold you back
from being social, such as negative thoughts, fears, or limiting beliefs. By freeing yourself from these anchors, you open yourself up to new possibilities and experiences.

It's also important to consider the role of virtual social networks in our lives. While nothing can replace in-person connections, virtual communities can provide support, inspiration, and networking opportunities. It's important to curate a virtual social network that aligns with your values and goals and to actively engage with it in a positive way.

So, in summary, to create extraordinary friendships, we need to choose our friends carefully, be the right kind of friend ourselves, get clear on our social values, stay positive, and actively nurture our relationships. With these principles in mind, we can build friendships that move and grow us, and make life so much richer and more fulfilling.

My Story

Looking back on my childhood experiences, I am filled with a sense of sadness and pain. As an only child, I felt like I was cut off from the world of socializing and interaction, and it was a lonely and isolating existence. I remember watching other children laughing and playing together, and I longed to be a part of their world.

But my first experience with friendship was not the warm and welcoming embrace that I had hoped for. Instead, it was a painful and hurtful encounter that left me feeling like I never quite fit in. I was seven years old. We were in a queue to use the restroom, and the girl next to me refused to hold my hand because she said my black skin would stick to hers. It was a crushing blow to my young spirit, and it made me feel like an outcast.

I remember going home that day and crying to myself, trying to make sense of why anyone would be so cruel. I never told anyone at home because emotions were not something that was discussed in my family. I had to try and make sense of everthing on my own.

I had to learn how to make friends, and it wasn't an easy process. It was a long and sometimes painful journey. Once a friend of mine approached me for financial assistance as she was being pursued by money-lenders. However, after borrowing the money, she refused to return it and instead resorted to spreading confidential information about my personal life in order to evade repayment.

As a result og multiple experience, I found that I was always a little hesitant to let people in. I had been hurt before, and I did not want to experience that pain again. But I also knew that I could not go through life without meaningful connections with others. So, I started to take small steps, opening up a little at a time, and finding people who accepted me for who I was.

But, today I am grateful for the very few close friends I have. They are people who see me, love me, and support me, no matter what. And while the scars of my childhood experiences still linger, they are reminders of how far I have come and how strong I am.

In building strong friendships, it's important to be there for each other and offer practical assistance when needed. Whether it's helping a friend move house or just being there to listen, small acts of kindness can go a long way in building strong bonds.

Finally, having mentors can be invaluable in helping us grow and achieve our goals. World-class mentors can offer guidance, support, and valuable insights into their own experiences. And with the advent of technology, we can also create a virtual social network of like-minded individuals who can offer support and inspiration.

In conclusion, building strong and positive friendships is an essential part of living a happy and fulfilled life. While it may not always be easy, it's important to be mindful of the kind of people we want in our lives and to surround ourselves with those who support and uplift us. By keeping a positive attitude, being there for each other, and striving to improve the quality of our social interactions, we can build strong and lasting friendships that enrich our lives.

The Plan:
Your Social Life

What are my social values?
I value positive, supportive, and uplifting relationships that encourage personal growth and mutual respect.

What is stopping me?
My toxic friend and negative social circle are hindering me from achieving the type of relationships that align with my social values.

Who is stopping me?
My toxic friend is a major obstacle to creating positive relationships, and my negative social circle reinforces my limiting beliefs and prevents me from branching out.

What type of social circle do I want?
I want a social circle that is optimistic, motivated, and supportive. A group of like-minded individuals who encourage each other to grow and achieve their goals.

Where will I find them?

- *Immediate – I can start by expanding my network on social media and joining groups that align with my interests and values*

- *Short-term – I can attend local events and join clubs or organizations that align with my passions to meet new people.*

- *Long-term – I can also work on building deeper connections with people I already know and trust, and focus on nurturing positive relationships with those who share similar values.*

STEP 7:
Your Intellecual Development

> *Two qualities are indispensable: first, an intellect that, even in the darkest hour, retains some glimmerings of the inner light which leads to truth; and second, the courage to follow this faint light wherever it may lead.*
>
> *- Carl von Clausewitz*

Intellectual development and lifelong learning are vital components of personal growth and happiness. It is said that a mind is a terrible thing to waste, and this could not be truer. From a young age, we are encouraged to learn and grow, but as we get older, it can be easy to fall into a rut and forget the importance of continued education.

The benefits of intellectual development and lifelong learning are immeasurable. From improving cognitive abilities to expanding career opportunities, the advantages of learning are endless. In fact, research has shown that engaging in intellectual pursuits can lead to increased life satisfaction and overall well-being.

Learning can take place in a variety of forms, including reading books, attending workshops and conferences, or engaging in discussions with others. The key is to maintain a hunger for knowledge and a willingness to learn and grow. By doing so, individuals can unlock their full potential and find purpose in their lives. This sense of purpose can lead to greater happiness and fulfilment.

Moreover, intellectual development is not limited to traditional academic settings. The ability to continuously discover new passions and interests is one of the greatest joys of lifelong learning. By keeping an open mind and a curious attitude, individuals can expand their knowledge and skills, enhancing their cognitive abilities, critical thinking skills, and ability to make informed decisions. Additionally, lifelong learning can foster creativity and innovation, as individuals gain new skills and knowledge that they can apply to their work and personal lives.

As individuals gain new skills and knowledge, they can feel a sense of accomplishment and pride in their abilities, leading to the development of self-confidence and self-esteem. This boost in confidence can lead to greater personal growth and achievement.

Lifelong learning can also help individuals adapt to changes and challenges in their personal and professional lives. By continually learning and growing, individuals become more resilient and better equipped to navigate obstacles and opportunities. Furthermore, lifelong learning can improve one's communication and interpersonal skills, leading to greater success in both personal and professional relationships.

In addition, lifelong learning can promote mental and emotional well-being. Engaging in activities such as reading, writing, and learning new skills can reduce stress and improve overall mood, providing a sense of purpose and fulfilment as individuals pursue their interests and passions.

Lifelong learning can also open up new career opportunities and increase earning potential. By staying up-to-date with industry trends and developments, individuals can become more competitive in the job market.

Beyond personal benefits, lifelong learning can also have a positive impact on society as a whole. By educating oneself, individuals can become informed and engaged citizens, contributing to the greater good of their communities and the world.

Moreover, lifelong learning can foster a sense of community and social connection. By engaging in learning activities and attending classes or workshops, individuals can meet new people with similar interests and build meaningful relationships.

Lifelong learning can also promote personal growth and self-discovery. By exploring new ideas and interests, individuals can gain a deeper understanding of themselves and their place in the world. This can lead to greater self-awareness and a stronger sense of identity.

Lastly, lifelong learning can be a source of enjoyment and personal fulfilment. By pursuing hobbies and interests, individuals can find joy and satisfaction in learning new things and challenging themselves. This can enhance their overall quality of life and well-being.

In summary, lifelong learning can have a significant positive impact on personal development, promoting knowledge acquisition, creativity, confidence, adaptability, communication, mental and emotional well-being, career advancement, personal growth, and enjoyment.

My Story

Growing up, I was constantly told in school that I was stupid. It seemed like every teacher I had didn't understand me and I didn't understand them. It wasn't the lesson itself that was the problem, but the environment in which I was expected to learn. Anytime I didn't like a teacher, I performed badly. It was like a self-fulfilling prophecy, and it only added to my feelings of inadequacy.

It's hard to describe just how devastating it is to feel like you're not smart enough. For me, it started in school, where I was constantly told that I wasn't good enough, that I wasn't smart enough, that I wasn't capable of achieving anything meaningful. It seemed like no matter how hard I tried, no matter how much effort I put in, it was never enough. I remember feeling so small, so insignificant, like I didn't matter at all.

It wasn't just my academic performance that suffered - it was my mental health too. I felt like a failure in every aspect of my life, and I didn't see any way out. It was like a vicious cycle - the more I failed, the worse I felt about myself, and the worse I felt about myself, the more I failed.

The impact of feeling stupid goes much deeper than just academic performance or career prospects. It affects our sense of self-worth, our confidence, and our ability to pursue our dreams. When we believe we're not smart enough, we stop ourselves from trying new things or taking on new challenges. We convince ourselves that we'll just fail anyway, so why bother?

As I progressed through my classes, I found myself getting more and more lost. The lessons didn't make sense, and I couldn't keep up with my peers. I felt so stupid and useless, like I was never going to be good at anything. These feelings of hopelessness and despair led to depression and even suicidal thoughts. I couldn't see a future for myself where I was successful or happy.

To make matters worse, I didn't have anyone to guide me through the lessons. The few teachers I did like were few and far between, and they were usually too busy to give me the individual attention I needed. It seemed like no one cared about my education or my future. I was left to struggle on my own, and I came to believe that if I really wanted something, I would fail at it.

It took me a long time to realize that it wasn't me who was the problem, but the system in which I was expected to learn. I had to find my own way to learn and grow, to find the things that interested me and pursue them with passion. I had to learn to believe in myself, even when no one else did.

Looking back, I can see how much I've grown and how far I've come. I'm no longer that scared, lost kid who felt like he would never amount to anything. I've found my passions and pursued them with vigour, and I've become a successful and confident person.

But I know that there are still so many others out there who are struggling, just like I was. They're told they're stupid or useless, and they feel like they'll never be able to succeed. My message to them is this: don't give up. You are not stupid or useless. You are capable of achieving great things, and you just need to find your own way to do it. Seek out the things that interest you, pursue them with passion, and never stop learning and growing. With hard work and perseverance, you can overcome any obstacle and achieve your dreams.

The Plan:
Your Intellectual Development

A) What have I been always good at?
I have always been good at drawing.

B) What do I enjoy doing the most?
I enjoy travelling the most.

C) What are some things that appear on both lists above?
Creating art inspired by my travels is something that appears on both lists.

What skills/knowledge do I lack to do the things in (C) better?
I lack the knowledge and skills in marketing, branding and entrepreneurship to turn my art into a successful business.

How can I gain these skills?

- *Immediate - I can start by researching online and reading books about marketing and entrepreneurship.*

- *Short-term - I can take online courses and attend workshops that focus on these skills.*

- *Long-term - I can consider going back to school to get a degree in business.*

What are the things that I must continue to do now (maybe a job)?
I am currently working as a clerk in accounting.

What skills/knowledge do I lack to do the things I must continue to do?
I lack the knowledge and skills in forensic accounting.

How can I gain these skills?

- Immediate - I can start by speaking with my manager and colleagues to learn more about the field.

- *Short-term - I can take online courses and attend workshops that focus on forensic accounting.*

- *Long-term - I can consider going back to school to get a degree in forensic accounting.*

Can I do both or must I transition from what I must do to what I want to do in (C)?
I can continue working as a clerk in accounting while pursuing my passion for creating art inspired by my travels.

What is my transition plan?

- Immediate - I can start by setting aside time every week to work on my art and research about entrepreneurship.

- Short-term - I can create a website to showcase my art and start selling my work online.

- Long-term - I can consider opening my own art studio or gallery to sell my work and showcase the work of other artists.

STEP 8:
Your Finances

> *If we command our wealth, we shall be rich and free; if our wealth commands us, we are poor indeed.*
>
> *- Edmund Burke*

Money, money, money - it's a topic that can bring about all kinds of emotions and opinions. Some people see it as the root of all evil, while others see it as the key to happiness. Personally, I believe that money is simply a tool that we use to standardize and store value. It's a way of exchanging goods and services, and it helps to keep our society functioning smoothly.

However, it's important to remember that the love of money is not the same as the love of human contribution. Sure, money can give us a certain level of comfort and security, but it's the contributions we make to the world and the people around us that truly bring us fulfilment and happiness. We should strive to use our money in a way that aligns with our values and goals, and that brings about positive change in the world.

In his book, "The 7 Habits of Highly Effective People," Stephen Covey famously said, "The main thing is to keep the main thing the main thing." When it comes to money, this means keeping our priorities in check and not allowing the pursuit of wealth to overshadow the things that truly matter in life, such as relationships, personal growth, and contributing to our communities. By using money as a tool to support these important aspects of our lives, we can find a sense of balance and fulfilment that goes beyond mere financial gain.

I've come to realize that everything I want in life, whether it's financial success, a fulfilling career, or amazing friendships, is ultimately a means to achieving happiness. Because let's face it, what's the point of having all these things if we're not happy?

For me, happiness is made up of two parts: the satisfaction that comes from the progressive accomplishments of worthy goals and the absolute contentment and gratefulness for the way things are right now.

The first part, the satisfaction that comes from the progressive accomplishments of worthy goals, is all about having a clear direction in life and working towards something that truly matters to me. It's about setting goals that excite me and then putting in the hard work and effort to achieve them. There's nothing quite like the feeling of accomplishing something that I've been working towards for a long time. It gives me a sense of purpose and fulfilment that is hard to replicate in any other way.

The second part, the absolute contentment and gratefulness for the way things are right now, is all about appreciating the present moment and finding joy in the little things. It's about being grateful for what I have, rather than constantly yearning for more. This doesn't mean that I'm complacent or that I don't have any aspirations for the future. It just means that I'm able to find happiness in the present moment, regardless of my circumstances.

Ultimately, I believe that happiness is not just a destination but a journey. It's something that I work towards every day by setting meaningful goals, being grateful for what I have, and finding joy in the little things. And while the journey may not always be easy, it's always worth it in the end.

I am grateful for what I have, but that doesn't mean I'm content to stay where I am. I fully intend to expand my financial life even more from here. I'm going to strive to create more value for others, whether it's through my work or through acts of kindness and generosity. And as a result, I know that more wealth and abundance will flow to me and my family every day.

But my focus isn't solely on accumulating more wealth. I want to enjoy every single minute of the process. I want to savour the journey and appreciate the lessons and opportunities that come my way. Money is a tool that can be used to improve our lives and the lives of those around us, but it's not the only thing that matters. Ultimately, it's the relationships we have and the moments we share that truly make life worth living.

My Story

As I sit down to write about my financial struggles, my heart feels heavy with the weight of my memories. It's not easy to relive the moments when I hit rock bottom and struggled to get back up. But I know that sharing my story might inspire others who are going through similar challenges.

I have been at the bottom many times in my life. I've failed in businesses, been deep in debt, and had no clue how I was going to survive. But perhaps the most painful part of my journey was the betrayal I faced from people I trusted. People who were supposed to have my back took advantage of my trust and took all my hard-earned money. I lost everything - my savings, my business, my shelter, and even my sense of self-worth.

Each time I hit rock bottom, I had to muster up the courage to start all over again. It was a steep climb towards rebuilding my life, and it was such a hard struggle. But even in the darkest moments, I knew that I had to keep going. I had to keep fighting for my dreams, for my happiness, and for my right to financial freedom.

It wasn't until later that I realized that I had my own right to happiness and my own right to control my money. I realised holding on to my money and not giving away that controlling right wasn't a sign of selfishness. And love doesnt mean giving control to someone over your whole life. I always thougth I wouldnt know how to manage money. I was too scared. So much technical things about money management didnt make sense to me. I had to get smart about my money, learn how to make sound decisions based on research and take control of my life. I had to figure out what I wanted in order to live a financially stable and fulfilling life.

The journey wasn't easy. It was full of setbacks, failures, and disap-pointments. But with each step forward, I gained a little more confidence, a little more knowledge, and a little more strength. I learned to trust myself and my instincts, to be resilient in the face of adversity, and to never give up on my dreams.

My business is just starting, and while I don't have the financial freedom I desire yet, I have a plan to get there. It hasn't been an easy road, but I've come to understand the value of having a clear vision and a solid plan in place. It's crucial to know what you want in life, to have a clear idea of what success looks like for you, and to take the necessary steps to get there. It takes time, patience, and hard work, but it's worth it in the end. And while I may not have reached my destination yet, I know that with determination, perseverance, and a well-executed plan, I will get there.

If you are going through a tough financial situation, know that you are not alone. Keep fighting for your dreams, keep working towards your goals, and never give up. With time, patience, and persistence, you too can overcome any obstacle and achieve the financial freedom you deserve.

The Plan:
Your Finances

Financial management is not just about making more money, it's about utilizing money as a tool of trade to standardize and store value. The love of money for the sake of having more can lead to greed and unhappiness. I refer again to Stephen Covey, "The main thing is to keep the main thing the main thing." Ultimately, the main thing that I want is to be happy, and everything else is just a means to that end. Happiness is made up of two parts: first, the satisfaction that comes from the progressive accomplishments of worthy goals, and second, the absolute contentment and gratefulness for the way things are right now.

To achieve financial success, it's important to focus on using money as a tool to achieve our worthy goals. This means identifying our priorities and ensuring that our financial decisions align with those priorities. We should also cultivate a mindset of contentment and gratitude, recognizing the value of what we have right now while striving towards our future goals. By finding a balance between progress and contentment, we can achieve financial success while also experiencing true happiness and fulfilment in our lives.

In as much detail, answer the following questions:

How much do I need to sustain myself daily?
$50 per day, including basic necessities such as food, housing, and transportation.

How much of this I can reduce?
I can try to reduce my daily expenses by bringing my own lunch to work, using public transportation instead of owning a car, and finding affordable housing options.

How much is my debt?
I currently have $10,000 in credit card debt.

How much am I going to pay myself monthly (savings)?
I will try to save at least 10% of my monthly income, which comes out to be $200 per month.

How much am I going to pay towards my debts?
I will allocate $500 per month towards paying off my credit card debt.

Are there any alternate sources of income I can pursue based on the previous chapter?
Yes, I can pursue freelance work or start a side hustle to supplement my income.

How much do I need to set aside for my education/training towards intellectual and career development?
I need to set aside $1,000 per year for training and education.

What does my financial plan look like now in a year?
In a year, I aim to have paid off at least half of my credit card debt, have saved $2,400 in my savings account, and have started working towards developing additional sources of income.

STEP 9:
Your Career

> *Climbing to the top demands strength, whether it is to the top of Mount Everest or to the top of your career.*
>
> *- A. P. J. Abdul Kalam*

What is the purpose of a successful, fulfilling career? A successful, fulfilling career serves as a way to fulfil one's potential and contribute to society. It provides a sense of purpose and direction in life, and can lead to financial stability and independence. For many people, their career is a large part of their identity, and achieving success in their chosen field can bring a great deal of personal satisfaction and self-esteem

In today's fast-paced and competitive world, the importance of career development cannot be overstated. It's not just about earning a pay check but finding a sense of purpose and fulfilment in one's work. To achieve this, one must find work they love. This means exploring their passions, skills, and values to identify the type of work that would bring them joy and fulfilment. For example, renowned chef and TV personality Anthony Bourdain found his love for food and storytelling, which led him to travel the world, try new cuisines, and share his experiences with others.

But finding work you love is not enough. To excel in any career, you must get good at what you do. This means developing the skills, knowledge, and expertise required to perform at the highest level. For example, Oprah Winfrey started as a radio host but didn't become the successful media mogul she is today until she honed her skills in public speaking, interviewing, and leadership.

In addition to excelling in one's career, making a significant contribution is essential to finding meaning and fulfilment in work. This means finding ways to use one's skills and talents to positively impact others and society as a whole. For example, Nobel Peace Prize winner Malala Yousafzai uses her voice and platform to advocate for girls' education and empowerment, making a significant contribution to the world.

Lastly, creating a reputation for oneself is critical for success in any career. This means building a strong personal brand, establishing a network of professional contacts, and showcasing one's achievements and expertise. For example, Elon Musk has created a reputation as an innovative and forward-thinking entrepreneur, which has helped him attract investors, customers, and employees to his various ventures.

Live on the edge of what I'm capable of achieving.

Living on the edge of what one is capable of achieving means pushing oneself out of their comfort zone and taking on challenges that may be daunting or even seemingly impossible. It is through taking risks and pushing oneself that true growth and development occur. This can be seen in the example of Elon Musk, who has pushed the boundaries of space travel with his company SpaceX, and has faced many setbacks and challenges along the way. However, his determination and willingness to take risks have led to numerous successes, such as the launch of the Falcon Heavy rocket in 2018.

There is no reverse gear, so I must push through.

In any career or life endeavour, there will inevitably be set-backs and failures. However, it is important to not give up or give in to discouragement. Instead, one must push through and continue to work towards their goals. This can be seen in the example of J.K. Rowling, who faced multiple rejections before finally getting her first Harry Potter book published. Despite the initial setbacks, she persisted and went on to become one of the most successful authors of all time.

Achieving my life vision is a step-by-step process of paying the price for every goal upon which my life vision rests.

Achieving a fulfilling career and life vision is not a one-time event, but rather a process that involves setting goals and working towards them over time. Each goal requires a price to be paid in terms of hard work, dedication, and sacrifice. For example, Steve Jobs, the co-founder of Apple, had a clear vision for his company and worked tirelessly to achieve it. He was known for his uncompromising work ethic and attention to detail, and his success was the result of years of hard work and perseverance.

Big challenges are built into the fabric of big accomplishments.

In order to achieve great things, one must be willing to take on big challenges. These challenges may seem overwhelming at first, but they are an essential part of achieving success. For example, Oprah Winfrey, one of the most successful media moguls in history, faced many challenges throughout her career. She grew up in poverty and faced numerous obstacles on her path to success. However, she persevered and took on big challenges, such as launching her own television network, OWN, which has become a huge success. It is through taking on these challenges that one can achieve greatness and make a significant impact in their chosen field.

My Story

I destroyed my career, and with it, I lost a part of myself. When things started to go wrong in my personal life, my career was the first to suffer. My partner had cheated on me, took all my money and left without any news, not even to his family. I was left with nothing but debt and shame and anger. I couldn't understand why this is happening to me for the second time. Then, the depression hit. It was like a wave that came crashing down on me, taking away all of my motivation and drive. It felt like I was being punished for something that wasn't even my fault. My psychiatrist gave me time off from work.

During this time, my Boss and some colleagues tried to get me fired. They tried everything, from giving me bad work performance review on the grounds I was away from work, to going as far as to call for a medical review to gauge if I'm fit for work. And it all failed and I was allowed back to work.

However the damage was done. The environment was beyond toxic. It was just dayas and days of them making me feel useless and stupid. I tried to talk to my HR department about it, but they brushed me off, telling me to "just get over it." My colleagues, sensing weakness, started to spread malicious rumours about me, making my already toxic work environment unbearable.

Despite the advice of my doctor, I couldn't be transferred to another vacancy. I felt trapped, like I was in a nightmare that I couldn't wake up from. I felt like I had hit rock bottom, and I couldn't see a way out. But, in my midlife, I knew that I couldn't just give up. I had to take back control and plan the second half of my life in terms of my career.

I was always a bit of a loner, so I never thought networking was that important. I was content with just keeping my head down and getting my work done. But it wasn't enough. My lack of connections left be without a support network to turn to in times of trouble.

I was lost, scared, and I cried a lot. It was a dark time, but it was also a turning point. I started to reflect on my life as a whole and realized that my career was just one part of it. I began to see that my struggles with depression and my toxic work environment were not unique to me. Many others out there were also suffering in silence, feeling hopeless and stuck.

That's when I knew I had to share my story and the strategies that helped me pull through. The purpose of a successful, fulfilling career, I learned, is not just about financial stability or personal fulfilment. It's about living on the edge of what I'm capable of achieving, even when the odds are stacked against me. It's about embracing the fact that there is no reverse gear and pushing forward, even when it feels like the world is against me. It's about paying the price for every goal upon which my life vision rests, no matter how challenging it may be.

The challenges are not just obstacles to overcome but are built into the fabric of the big accomplishments that await on the other side. I know it's not easy, and it's a step-by-step process, but it's worth it. It's worth it to have a career that aligns with my values, to do work that I love, and to make a significant contribution. It's worth it to create a reputation for myself and to know that I'm making a difference in the world.

So, to anyone out there struggling with depression and feeling hopeless in their careers, I want you to know that there is a way out. You don't have to go through it alone. Reach out to someone you trust, seek help from a professional, and start taking small steps towards your goals. It may not be easy, but it's possible. Remember, big challenges lead to big accomplishments, and you're capable of achieving anything you set your mind to.

The Plan:
Your Career

Keeping in mind what career choice you identified under the chapter of intellectual development, you need to identify the gaps between where you are and where you want to be.

Where am I now?
Currently working as an accounting clerk
Limited experience and knowledge in art

Where do I want to be?
Pursuing a career in art, creating and selling my own artwork
Developing my skills and knowledge in art to create high-qual-ity work

Why do I want to be here? What about it do I like?
I have always had a passion for art and creating things with my hands
I want to express my creativity and share my art with others
I want to have a fulfilling career doing something that I love

What are my gaps?
Lack of formal education in art
Limited portfolio of artwork
Limited knowledge of how to market and sell artwork

How much time do I give myself?
1 year

What are my steps?

- *Assess my current financial situation and create a budget for the transition period: 2 weeks*

- *Research the art industry and identify potential markets for my artwork: 3 weeks*

- *Enrol in art courses to improve my skills and gain new techniques: 12 weeks*

- *Develop a daily art practice to create a consistent body of work for my portfolio: Ongoing*

- *Start building a portfolio of my artwork to showcase my skills: 4 weeks*

- *Invest in the necessary art supplies and equipment: 2 weeks*

- *Attend art exhibitions and fairs to network and gain exposure: 8 weeks*

- *Join art associations and online communities to connect with other artists and potential clients: Ongoing*

- *Collaborate with other artists to gain exposure and learn from their experiences: Ongoing*

- *Create an online portfolio and start promoting my artwork on social media: 4 weeks*

- *Develop a strong personal brand and unique style in my artwork: Ongoing*

- *Develop a pricing strategy for my artwork based on market research and the value of my skills: 3 weeks*

- *Create a business plan for my art career, including marketing and financial strategies: 6 weeks*

- *Identify potential sources of funding or grants for my art business: 2 weeks*

- *Attend workshops and seminars on art entrepreneurship and business management: 4 weeks*

- *Start offering art classes and workshops to supplement my income: 8 weeks*

- *Consider offering art commissions and personalized artwork to clients: Ongoing*

- *Attend art shows and exhibitions to network and gain exposure: 8 weeks*

- *Connect with art galleries and curators to potentially display my artwork: 6 weeks*

- *Stay committed to my art career and be open to new opportunities and challenges: Ongoing*

Note that some of these items are ongoing and may not have a specific time frame. This is just a rough estimate to help create a Gantt chart.

STEP 10:
Your Love Life

> *Being deeply loved by someone gives you strength, while loving someone deeply gives you courage.*
>
> — Lao Tzu

When it comes to envisioning a happy life, one cannot ignore the importance of love and companionship. Love is a powerful force that can transform our lives in countless ways, but it requires an extraordinary person to truly experience an extraordinary love. So, the question we must ask ourselves is: am I that person?

Love is not just a feeling, it is also an action. It requires effort, commitment, and sacrifice. To truly love someone, we must be willing to see them as valuable and worthy of our time and attention. We must be willing to put their needs before our own and to work through the challenges that come with any relationship.

But before we can love someone else, we must first love ourselves. We must understand our own worth and value as a person. This means taking care of ourselves physically, emotionally, and spiritually. We must also be willing to work on our flaws and insecurities, so that we can be the best possible version of ourselves.

When it comes to finding a partner, it's important to understand the kind of person we want to be with and the kind of partner we can be. We must be honest with ourselves about our strengths and weaknesses, and be willing to accept and work on them. It's also important to have a clear idea of our values and priorities, so that we can find someone who shares them.

In any relationship, it is important to have a clear understanding of what both partners want to achieve together. This shared vision is the foundation upon which the relationship is built. Without it, the relationship is likely to flounder and eventually fail. Therefore, it is essential for both partners to work together to define their joint vision and to understand what they need to do to achieve it.

Of course, finding the right partner is not always easy. It requires patience, resilience, and a willingness to put ourselves out there. We may face rejection or disappointment along the way, but we must keep in mind that the right person is worth the wait.

Dr Nathaniel Branden, a psychologist and author, defined love as "a passionate, spiritual, emotional, sexual attachment between two people that reflects a high regard for the value of each other's person." This definition reminds us that love is not just about physical attraction or emotional connection, but also about seeing the other person as valuable and worthy of respect.

In order to experience this kind of love, we must be willing to put in the work. We must be willing to be vulnerable, to communicate openly and honestly, and to make the effort to understand and appreciate our partner's perspective. We must also be willing to make sacrifices and compromises, to support and encourage each other, and to grow and evolve together.

At the end of the day, love is one of the most important things we can experience in life. It has the power to transform us, to bring us joy and fulfilment, and to give us a sense of purpose and meaning. But it requires us to be extraordinary people who are willing to put in the effort and take the risks necessary to experience an extraordinary love.

When partners work together to define their joint vision, they are essentially creating a roadmap for their relationship. This roadmap serves as a guide, helping both partners to stay on track and to make decisions that are aligned with their shared goals. It also helps to ensure that both partners are clear about what they want and what they are willing to do to achieve it.

Defining a joint vision requires a great deal of communication and collaboration. It requires partners to be open and honest with each other about their hopes, dreams, and aspirations. It also requires them to be willing to compromise and to make sacrifices for the sake of the relationship.

When partners have a clear understanding of their joint vision, they are better able to understand what they need to contribute to the relationship. They are able to identify their strengths and weaknesses and to determine how they can best support their partner in achieving their shared goals. This understanding is essential for creating a strong and healthy relationship.

In addition, understanding the joint vision also helps partners to understand what they would like their partner to bring into the relationship. They are able to identify the qualities and characteristics that are important to them and to communicate these to their partner. This helps to ensure that both partners are on the same page and that they are working together towards a common goal.

Ultimately, understanding the joint vision is key to creating a successful and fulfilling relationship. It helps partners to stay focused on their shared goals and to support each other in achieving them. It also helps to ensure that both partners are clear about their expectations and that they are working together towards a common goal. By taking the time to define their joint vision, partners can create a strong and healthy relationship that will stand the test of time.

My Story

Love is a complex emotion that can take us to the heights of happiness and also leave us in the depths of despair. For me, love has been a rollercoaster ride that has left me broken and in debt. I have loved only twice in my life, and both times, I was left with a shattered heart and a drained bank account. My first love was three times my age, and he was the first person to ever say "I love you" to me. I was coming from a broken place where I hated myself, and I clung to him as if he were my lifeline. He was of a similar background to me but from a different country, and I thought we had a deep connection. But lhe never worked a day in his life, and he cheated on me with other women. I was left with nothing but debt and a broken heart.

My second love was seven years my junior, and I thought he was the one for me. He was of a different background but local to where I lived, and I thought we could build a life together. But once again, I was wrong. He too cheated on me and left me with nothing but debt. I remember one time when I didn't have enough money to change my broken shoe, but my partner wanted a new shirt. I gave him the money instead. Months later, he told me that his girlfriend was pregnant, and he wanted me to accommodate her into our relationship. Funnily enough, I tried to adjust, but looking back, I realized that it was all my broken parts that were making me do this.

I had not formed my own identity, and I felt I needed to earn love. I didn't realize how much I was sacrificing for my partners, and I didn't realize my worth in the relationship. I was empty and broken, and I needed someone else to complete me. But the truth is, I needed to complete myself first. I needed to know myself, have my boundaries, and know what kind of partner I was. I needed to expect equality from my partner, not just in terms of material wealth, but also in terms of love and care.

These experiences have taught me that love is not just about giving everything you have and sacrificing everything for your partner. It's about knowing yourself, respecting your own boundaries, and expecting the same from your partner. It's about understanding the things that truly matter to you in a relationship and not settling for anything less. It's about building a relationship on a foundation of mutual love and respect, where both partners support and uplift each other.

My struggles in love have inspired me to share my story with others so that they can avoid making the same mistakes I did. I want people to know that they deserve love and respect, and they should never settle for anything less. I want them to know that love is not about sacrifice and giving everything, you have. It's about finding someone who complements you and supports you in your journey of self-discovery and growth. I urge everyone to take the time to know themselves, set their boundaries, and expect equality from their partners. Only then can we build relationships that are truly fulfilling and bring us the happiness we deserve.

The Plan:
Your Love Life

The quest for love is a universal human desire, and finding that special someone who ignites passion and connection is an extraordinary experience. However, the road to finding extraordinary love requires extraordinary effort and introspection. To attract an extraordinary partner, one must first ask oneself if they are an extraordinary person. Love requires action, and it is up to each individual to invest in personal growth and development. Remember what Dr Nathaniel Branden said, "extraordinary love requires a passionate, spiritual, emotional, and sexual attachment between two people that reflects a high regard for the value of each other's person". To create such a relationship, one must be willing to act, commit to personal growth, and foster a deep appreciation for one's partner.

What kinds of loving relationship do I want?
I want a loving relationship that is based on mutual respect, trust, and open communication. I want a partner who is supportive of my goals and dreams and who is willing to grow and evolve together with me. I also want a relationship that is passionate and intimate, with a strong emotional connection.

What is the ultimate goal of my relationship?
The ultimate goal of my relationship is to create a lifelong partnership that is fulfilling, supportive, and brings out the best in both of us. I want to build a life with my partner that is full of joy, love, and shared experiences. I believe that our relationship should be a source of strength and inspiration for us both, allowing us to reach our full potential and achieve our goals.

What values and habits to I have that makes me an extraordinary lover?

- *I prioritize open communication and actively listen to my partner's needs and concerns.*

- *I show affection and appreciation through small gestures like thoughtful gifts or surprise dates.*

- *I try to learn and understand my partner's love language to better meet their emotional needs.*

- *I am committed to personal growth and self-improvement to become the best version of myself for my partner.*

- *I prioritize quality time and make sure to carve out time in my schedule for dates and special moments together.*

- *I am honest and transparent in my thoughts and feelings, even when it's uncomfortable.*

- *I try to learn about and support my partner's interests and passions.*

- *I am respectful of my partner's boundaries and make sure to establish and honour my own.*

- *I prioritize trust and strive to maintain a strong foundation of honesty and loyalty in the relationship.*

- *I am committed to working through challenges and conflicts in a healthy and constructive way to strengthen the relationship.*

What values and habits that I lack in becoming an extraordinary lover?

- *I might not always be as patient as I could be when it comes to listening to my partner's needs and concerns.*

- *I could make more of an effort to surprise my partner with thoughtful gestures, such as leaving little notes of appreciation or planning a surprise outing.*

- *I might not always be aware of or fully understand my partner's love language, and could work to better learn and implement it in our relationship.*

- *I could focus more on specific areas of personal growth and self-improvement that directly relate to my partner's needs and desires.*

- *I might occasionally prioritize other obligations over quality time with my partner, and could make more of an effort to prioritize our relationship.*

- *I could work on being more vulnerable and transparent in expressing my thoughts and feelings, especially when they may be difficult to share.*

- *I might not always make enough of an effort to learn about and support my partner's interests and passions.*

- *I could sometimes be more considerate of my partner's boundaries, especially in situations where they might conflict with my own desires.*

- *I might occasionally struggle with trusting my partner fully, and could work on building that trust through ongoing communication and transparency.*

- *I could work on being more proactive in addressing conflicts and challenges in our relationship, rather than letting them simmer or avoiding them altogether.*

What values & habits do I seek in my partner?

- *Honesty and transparency in communication and actions.*

- *Emotional intelligence and the ability to effectively communicate their feelings.*

- *A strong sense of self and personal identity outside of the relationship.*

- *Respect for personal boundaries and a willingness to establish and honour my own.*

- *A shared commitment to personal growth and self-improvement.*

- *The ability to prioritize quality time and try to maintain the relationship.*

- *Shared values and beliefs about the importance of trust and loyalty in a relationship.*

- *A willingness to work through challenges and conflicts in a healthy and constructive way.*

- *Support for my interests and passions and a willingness to learn and engage with them.*

- *A deep appreciation and regard for my person and value as a partner.*

BRINGING IT ALL TOGETHER:
Part A - A Clear Visison

Success is something that many people aspire to achieve in their lives. Whether it's in their personal relationships, their careers, their health, or their finances, people often work hard to reach their goals and experience the satisfaction that comes with accomplishing something meaningful. However, the benefits of success go far beyond just achieving one specific goal. In fact, creating and achieving success in any area of your life can fuel, charge, and move your whole life forward, as it spills over into the overall quality of your life.

When you accomplish something significant, it has a ripple effect on the other areas of your life. For example, if you achieve a promotion at work, you might feel more confident in your abilities and have a greater sense of financial security, which can positively impact your personal relationships and your health. If you lose weight and get in better shape, you might feel more energized and motivated in other areas of your life, such as your career or your hobbies.

This spill over effect is what makes achieving success in one area of your life so valuable. When you invest time and effort into improving one aspect of your life, you'll likely see improvements in other areas as well. For example, if you work on improving your communication skills in your personal relationships, you might find that you're more effective in your professional communication as well.

However, it's important to remember that each category of your life is mandatory to be worked on. You can't neglect one area of your life and expect to achieve success in another. For example, if you're focused solely on your career and neglecting your health, you might find that your success at work is ultimately hampered by health problems or burnout.

It's also important to have a plan for your life. Most people fail to plan their lives and instead simply react to whatever comes their way. But if you want to achieve success in multiple areas of your life, you need to have a clear idea of what you want to accomplish and how you're going to get there. This means setting goals, creating a timeline, and acting to make your dreams a reality.

In order to create a plan for your life, you first need to identify what's important to you. This might include your career, your relationships, your health, your finances, your spirituality, or any number of other areas. Once you know what's important to you, you can set specific goals for each area of your life and create a plan to achieve them.

When creating your plan, it's important to be realistic about what you can accomplish and to break your goals down into smaller, more manageable steps. This will help you stay motivated and make progress towards your goals, even when the going gets tough.

It's also important to hold yourself accountable for your progress. This might mean tracking your progress towards your goals, seeking feedback from others, or working with a coach or mentor who can help you stay on track.

Another key factor in achieving success in multiple areas of your life is to set boundaries and create balance. It's easy to get caught up in one area of your life and neglect others, but this can ultimately lead to burnout, stress, and even failure. By setting boundaries and creating balance, you can ensure that you're giving each area of your life the attention it deserves.

Creating success in multiple areas of your life isn't easy, but it's worth the effort. By investing in yourself and acting to achieve your goals, you can improve the overall quality of your life and experience greater satisfaction and fulfilment.

However, most people fail to plan like Alice:

Alice: "Would you tell me, please, which way I ought to go from here?"

The Cheshire Cat: "That depends a good deal on where you want to get to."

Alice: "I don't much care where."

The Cheshire Cat: "Then it doesn't much matter which way you go."

Alice: "...so long as I get somewhere."

The Cheshire Cat: "Oh, you're sure to do that, if only you walk long enough."

Our ability to envision the future is what separates us from other animals. We have the power to imagine a future that does not yet exist and then work towards making it a reality. A clear and compelling life vision is crucial for living a fulfilling and meaningful life. It is the mental image of what the future will or could look like, and it serves as a roadmap for our decisions and actions.

Without a clear vision, our decision-making process is reduced to the simple calculus of pleasure and pain. We become reactive rather than proactive, making choices based on immediate gratification rather than long-term consequences. This short-sightedness can lead to a life of regret and unfulfillment.

In contrast, a well-crafted life vision can give us the clarity and purpose we need to make the right choices. It helps us to tolerate the pain of the moment, knowing that the long-term pleasure is worth the sacrifice. We can be intentional and proactive, creating a life that aligns with our values and aspirations.

The process of creating a life vision starts with self-reflection. We need to take a step back and assess our lives as they are right now. What do we value? What are our strengths and weaknesses? What are our passions and interests? What brings us joy and fulfilment?

Once we have a clear understanding of ourselves, we can start to envision what we want our future to look like. This process involves dreaming big and allowing ourselves to imagine what could be possible. We should let go of any limiting beliefs or self-doubt and create a mental picture of our ideal life.

The life vision we create should be compelling and motivating. It should be something that excites us and gives us a sense of purpose. It should inspire us to act and make the necessary changes to achieve our goals.

However, it's important to remember that creating a life vision is just the first step. It's essential to break down our vision into actionable steps and set realistic goals to achieve it. We need to develop a plan and take consistent action towards our goals.

Another crucial aspect of creating a life vision is to remain flexible and adaptable. Life is unpredictable, and we need to be able to adjust our vision and goals as circumstances change. It's okay if our vision evolves over time, as long as we remain true to our values and aspirations.

Moreover, it's important to recognize that creating a life vision is not a one-time event. It's an ongoing process that requires regular reflection and adjustment. We need to continuously assess our progress and make any necessary changes to ensure that our life is aligned with our vision.

In conclusion, our ability to envision the future is what sets us apart from other animals. A clear and compelling life vision is crucial for living a fulfilling and meaningful life. It helps us to make the right choices and gives us a sense of purpose and direction. However, creating a life vision is just the first step. We need to break down our vision into actionable steps and remain flexible and adaptable as circumstances change. By doing so, we can live a life that aligns with our values and aspirations, and that is truly fulfilling.

The Plan:
A Hollistic Vision

For each of the component, list 6 goals maximum, and for each goal state why you want this goal and the negative impact of not achieving it.

Your thoughts:

1. Meditate daily for 10 minutes to improve focus and mindfulness.

Why I want this:
Meditation can improve my mental and emotional well-being by reducing stress and anxiety, enhancing focus and attention, and increasing self-awareness.

What's the impact of not doing anything about this?
Without meditation, I may struggle to manage stress and anxiety, leading to negative impacts on my mental health and overall well-being.

2. Read at least one book per month to broaden knowledge and perspectives.

Why I want this:

Reading can broaden my knowledge and perspectives, enhance my creativity, and stimulate my imagination. It can also improve my communication skills and reduce stress.

What's the impact of not doing anything about this?
Without reading regularly, I may miss out on valuable insights and ideas, limiting my personal and professional growth.

3. Attend a critical thinking or problem-solving workshop to enhance analytical skills.

Why I want this:
Critical thinking and problem-solving skills are essential for making sound decisions and solving complex problems. Attending a workshop can provide me with practical tools and strategies to approach problems in a systematic and logical way.

What's the impact of not doing anything about this?
Without improving my critical thinking and problem-solving skills, I may struggle to make effective decisions and miss opportunities for growth and success.

4. Take a course in a new language to expand linguistic capabilities.

Why I want this:
Learning a new language can broaden my horizons, expand my cultural understanding, and improve my cognitive function. It can also enhance my career prospects and provide new opportunities for travel and personal growth.

What's the impact of not doing anything about this?
Without learning a new language, I may miss out on valuable connections and experiences in other cultures, limiting my personal and professional growth.

5.   Practice positive self-talk to improve self-esteem and mental health.

Why I want this:
Positive self-talk can improve my self-esteem and mental health, increase my resilience, and help me develop a more optimistic outlook on life.

What's the impact of not doing anything about this?
Without practicing positive self-talk, I may struggle with negative self-talk and low self-esteem, leading to negative impacts on my mental and emotional well-being.

6.   Participate in a debate or discussion group to sharpen communication skills.

Why I want this:
Debating and discussing with others can improve my communication skills, enhance my ability to articulate my thoughts and ideas, and provide new insights and perspectives.

What's the impact of not doing anything about this?
Without participating in debates or discussions, I may struggle to communicate effectively with others, miss out on valuable insights and perspectives, and limit my personal and professional growth.

Your emotions:

1.   Attend a therapy session to work through past trauma or emotional barriers.

Why I want this:
I want to address and heal any unresolved emotional wounds or trauma from my past that may be affecting my present well-being and relationships.

What's the impact of not doing anything about this?
The impact of not addressing past trauma or emotional barriers is the potential for ongoing emotional distress, difficulty forming healthy relationships, and a negative impact on overall mental health.

2. Practice forgiveness and letting go of grudges towards others.
Why I want this:

I want to cultivate emotional maturity, develop empathy and understanding, and create more positive relationships with others.

What's the impact of not doing anything about this?
The impact of holding onto grudges and refusing to forgive others is ongoing negative emotions such as anger and resentment, strained relationships, and potential mental and physical health issues.

3. Practice self-compassion and self-love by prioritizing self-care.

Why I want this:
I want to improve my self-esteem and mental health by prioritizing my own needs and taking care of myself.

What's the impact of not doing anything about this?
The impact of not prioritizing self-care and self-love can lead to feelings of burnout, exhaustion, and low self-esteem, potentially affecting overall physical and mental health.

4. Attend a communication workshop to improve emotional expression and listening skills.

Why I want this:
I want to enhance my ability to effectively communicate with others, express emotions, and actively listen to others, leading to better relationships and understanding.
What's the impact of not doing anything about this?
The impact of not improving communication skills can lead to misunderstandings, conflicts, and difficulty forming positive relationships with others.

5. *Identify and address triggers for negative emotions such as anger or anxiety.*

Why I want this:
I want to better understand and manage my own emotions, leading to more emotional stability and better relationships with others.

What's the impact of not doing anything about this?
The impact of not addressing triggers for negative emotions can lead to emotional outbursts, strained relationships, and potentially long-term mental and physical health issues.

6. *Seek feedback from others on emotional intelligence and work on areas for improvement.*

Why I want this:
I want to improve my emotional intelligence, develop stronger relationships with others, and enhance my overall well-being.

What's the impact of not doing anything about this?
The impact of not seeking feedback and improving emotional intelligence can lead to difficulty relating to others, strained relationships, and a negative impact on overall mental and emotional health.

Your personal character:

1. *Practice honesty and integrity in all interactions with others.*

Why I want this:
I want to be known as a person with a strong moral character and gain the trust and respect of others.

What's the impact of not doing anything about this?
If I don't practice honesty and integrity, I may damage my reputation and relationships with others, leading to a lack of trust and respect.

2. *Volunteer regularly to develop a sense of empathy and compassion towards others.*

Why I want this:
I want to develop a deeper understanding of others' experiences and develop a greater sense of compassion towards those in need.

 What's the impact of not doing anything about this?
If I don't volunteer, I may become more self-centred and less connected to the needs of others, leading to a lack of empathy and compassion.

3. *Set boundaries and practice assertiveness to develop confidence and self-respect.*

Why I want this:
I want to feel confident and respected in my interactions with others and be able to advocate for my needs.

What's the impact of not doing anything about this?
If I don't set boundaries and practice assertiveness, I may allow others to take advantage of me, leading to feelings of resentment and a lack of self-respect.

4. Take responsibility for mistakes and actively work to improve personal weaknesses.

Why I want this:
I want to become a better person and continually improve myself.

What's the impact of not doing anything about this?
If I don't take responsibility for my mistakes and work to improve myself, I may continue to make the same mistakes and fail to reach my full potential.

5. Practice gratitude and positivity in daily life to develop a sense of contentment and appreciation.

Why I want this:
I want to cultivate a positive outlook on life and feel more satisfied with what I have.

What's the impact of not doing anything about this?
If I don't practice gratitude and positivity, I may become more negative and dissatisfied with my life, leading to a lack of fulfilment and happiness.

6. Engage in acts of kindness and generosity towards others to develop a sense of altruism.

Why I want this:
I want to develop a greater sense of compassion and care for others and make a positive impact in the world.

What's the impact of not doing anything about this?
If I don't engage in acts of kindness and generosity, I may become more self-centred and less connected to the needs of others, leading to a lack of fulfilment and purpose in life.

Your spiritual self:

1. Attend a religious service or practice meditation to connect with a higher power or inner self.

Why I want this:
I want to develop a deeper sense of spirituality and connect with a higher power or inner self. This can provide a sense of purpose and meaning, as well as a source of comfort and guidance in difficult times.

What's the impact of not doing anything about this?
I may feel a lack of connection and direction in life, and may struggle to find meaning and purpose in challenging situations.

2. Read spiritual texts or attend workshops to deepen understanding of spiritual beliefs.

Why I want this:
I want to deepen my understanding of spiritual beliefs and practices in order to live a more meaningful and purposeful life. This can also provide a sense of community and connection with others who share similar beliefs.

What's the impact of not doing anything about this?
I may miss out on the wisdom and guidance provided by spiritual texts and teachings, and may feel a lack of connection with others who share similar beliefs.

3. Practice mindfulness and self-reflection to develop a sense of inner peace and clarity.

Why I want this:
I want to develop a greater sense of inner peace and clarity, which can help me navigate life's challenges with greater ease and resilience. Mindfulness and self-reflection can also help me gain insight into my own thoughts and emotions, and improve my relationships with others.

What's the impact of not doing anything about this?
I may feel overwhelmed or stressed by life's challenges, and may struggle to manage my thoughts and emotions in a healthy way. This can lead to difficulties in relationships and a sense of disconnection from self and others.

4. Practice gratitude and appreciation for life's blessings.

Why I want this:
I want to cultivate a sense of gratitude and appreciation for the blessings in my life, which can increase my overall sense of well-being and happiness. This can also help me focus on the positive aspects of life, even during difficult times.

What's the impact of not doing anything about this?
I may feel a sense of negativity or discontentment with life, and may struggle to find joy or fulfilment in day-to-day experiences.

5. Practice forgiveness and compassion towards self and others.

Why I want this:
I want to cultivate a sense of forgiveness and compassion towards myself and others, which can improve my relationships and overall sense of well-being. This can also help me release negative emotions and move forward in a positive way.

What's the impact of not doing anything about this?
I may hold onto resentment or negative emotions towards my-self or others, which can lead to strained relationships and a sense of emotional heaviness.

6. Participate in acts of service or volunteer work to develop a sense of purpose and meaning.

Why I want this:
I want to participate in acts of service or volunteer work in order to make a positive impact on the world and develop a greater sense of purpose and meaning in my own life. This can also provide a sense of connection with others and a greater understanding of the needs of different communities.

What's the impact of not doing anything about this?
I may miss out on the opportunity to make a positive impact on the world and may struggle to find a sense of purpose or meaning in my own life.

Your physical wellness:

1. Set a goal to exercise for at least 30 minutes per day to im-prove physical health.

Why I want this?
Regular exercise has numerous health benefits, such as improv-ing cardiovascular health, reducing the risk of chronic diseases, and improving mood and energy levels.
What's the impact of not doing anything about this?
Failing to exercise regularly can lead to weight gain, increased risk of chronic diseases such as diabetes and heart disease, decreased energy levels, and increased risk of mental health issues such as anxiety and depression.

2. Make a commitment to eat a balanced diet with a focus on whole foods and minimal processed foods.

Why I want this?
Eating a balanced diet with whole foods provides the necessary nutrients for the body to function properly and helps maintain a healthy weight.

What's the impact of not doing anything about this?
Poor nutrition can lead to a range of health problems such as obesity, malnutrition, and chronic diseases such as heart disease and diabetes.

3. Practice stress-reducing activities such as yoga or meditation to improve mental and physical health.

Why I want this?
Stress is a common issue that can negatively impact both mental and physical health, and practicing stress-reducing activities can improve overall well-being.

What's the impact of not doing anything about this?
Failure to manage stress can lead to chronic health problems such as hypertension, anxiety disorders, and depression.

4. Get regular check-ups and preventative care to maintain physical health.

Why I want this?
Regular check-ups and preventative care can catch health issues early, making them easier to treat, and prevent potential health problems from developing.

What's the impact of not doing anything about this?
Neglecting preventative care can lead to undetected health problems that may escalate into more serious conditions, requiring more invasive and impactful treatments.

5. Practice good sleep hygiene to ensure adequate rest and recovery.

Why I want this?
Adequate sleep is essential for mental and physical health, as it allows the body to rest and recover, promotes memory consolidation, and regulates mood.

What's the impact of not doing anything about this?
Inadequate sleep can lead to a range of issues such as fatigue, reduced productivity, and increased risk of accidents, and long-term sleep deprivation has been linked to chronic health problems such as obesity, diabetes, and heart disease.

6. Make a commitment to reduce or eliminate harmful habits such as smoking or excessive alcohol consumption.

Why I want this?
Harmful habits such as smoking and excessive alcohol consumption can have severe negative impacts on physical and mental health and lead to addiction.

What's the impact of not doing anything about this?
The negative health consequences of smoking and excessive alcohol consumption are well documented, and can lead to a range of issues such as respiratory problems, liver disease, and cancer. Additionally, addiction to these substances can be impactful, damaging personal relationships and impacting job performance.

Your social life:

1. Join a social group or club to expand social circle and network.

Why I want this:
To increase social opportunities and connect with like-minded individuals.

What's the impact of not doing anything about this?
Stagnant social life and limited networking opportunities, which can lead to feelings of loneliness and isolation.

2. Make a commitment to spend time with friends and family regularly.

Why I want this:
To maintain close relationships with loved ones and support systems.

What's the impact of not doing anything about this?
Neglecting relationships with friends and family can lead to strained relationships and a lack of emotional support.

3. Attend social events or networking opportunities to develop social skills and connections.

Why I want this:
To develop social skills and build a professional network.
What's the impact of not doing anything about this?

Missed opportunities for personal and professional growth, and limited social and career prospects.

4. Practice active listening and effective communication skills in social interactions.

Why I want this:
To improve communication and foster stronger relationships with others.

What's the impact of not doing anything about this?
Poor communication can lead to misunderstandings, conflict, and damaged relationships.

5. Work on conflict resolution skills to maintain positive relationships with others.

Why I want this:
To maintain positive relationships with friends, family, and colleagues.

What's the impact of not doing anything about this?
Poor conflict resolution skills can lead to unresolved issues, tension, and damaged relationships.

6. Engage in acts of service or volunteer work to develop a sense of community and social responsibility.

Why I want this:
To give back to the community and develop a sense of purpose.

What's the impact of not doing anything about this?
Missed opportunities to make a positive impact on the community and develop a sense of social responsibility.

Your intellectual development:

1. Take a course or workshop in a new subject or skill to broaden intellectual horizons.

Why I want this?
Learning new subjects or skills helps to expand our knowledge and capabilities, and allows us to explore our interests and passions.

What's the impact of not doing anything about this?
Sticking to what we already know can lead to stagnation and a lack of personal growth, limiting our potential in both personal and professional spheres.

2. Read widely and regularly to expand knowledge and understanding of diverse topics.

Why I want this?
Reading regularly helps to broaden our perspective and understanding of the world, exposing us to diverse cultures, ideas, and experiences.

What's the impact of not doing anything about this?
Failing to read widely can lead to a narrow worldview and a lack of empathy towards others who may hold different beliefs or experiences.

3. Engage in critical thinking and problem-solving activities to develop analytical skills.

Why I want this?
Developing analytical skills helps to improve decision-making, problem-solving, and overall cognitive abilities, enabling us to approach challenges with a more logical and efficient mindset.

What's the impact of not doing anything about this?

Failing to engage in critical thinking can lead to poor decision-making, lack of creativity, and limited problem-solving skills.

4. *Attend lectures or talks on topics of interest to deepen understanding and engagement.*

Why I want this?
Attending lectures or talks helps to deepen understanding of topics of interest, and provides opportunities for intellectual engagement with others who share similar interests.

What's the impact of not doing anything about this?
Failing to attend lectures or talks can limit exposure to new ideas and perspectives, and limit opportunities for networking and collaboration with like-minded individuals.

5. *Practice creative pursuits such as writing, art, or music to develop imagination and innovation.*

Why I want this?
Engaging in creative pursuits helps to develop imagination, innovation, and self-expression, providing an outlet for personal growth and exploration.

What's the impact of not doing anything about this?
Failing to engage in creative pursuits can limit personal growth and self-expression, leading to a lack of fulfilment and creativity in life.

*6. Seek out opportunities for mentorship or apprenticeship
to learn from experts in a field of interest.*

Why I want this?

*Seeking mentorship or apprenticeship opportunities helps to
learn from experts in a field of interest, providing guidance
and insight to improve skills and knowledge.*

What's the impact of not doing anything about this?
*Failing to seek out mentorship or apprenticeship can limit
personal and professional growth, and hinder the development of new skills and knowledge in a chosen field.*

Financial planning and management:

*1. Set a budget and financial goals for short-term and long-
term planning.*

Why I want this?
*By setting a budget and financial goals, I can have better con-
trol over my spending and work towards achieving my financial objectives.*

What's the impact of not doing anything about this?
*Without a budget and financial goals, I may overspend, have
no clear direction on how to allocate my funds, and struggle to
achieve my financial objectives.*

*2. Review and update financial accounts and investments
regularly.*

Why I want this?
*Regularly reviewing and updating my financial accounts and
investments can help me to make informed decisions, identify
potential issues early on, and adjust my strategy as needed.*

What's the impact of not doing anything about this?
If I don't review and update my financial accounts and investments regularly, I may miss out on potential opportunities or run into financial issues that could have been avoided.

3. Practice responsible spending and saving habits to ensure financial stability.

Why I want this?
By practicing responsible spending and saving habits, I can achieve financial stability, reduce financial stress, and have more financial freedom in the future.

What's the impact of not doing anything about this?
Without responsible spending and saving habits, I may struggle with debt, overspending, and lack of financial stability, which can negatively impact my overall well-being.

4. Work on reducing debt and improving credit score.

Why I want this?
By reducing debt and improving my credit score, I can increase my financial options, qualify for better loan terms and interest rates, and ultimately save money in the long run.

What's the impact of not doing anything about this?
If I don't work on reducing debt and improving my credit score, I may be limited in my financial options, struggle to qualify for loans or credit cards, and pay higher interest rates.

5. Increase financial literacy by reading books, attending seminars or taking courses on personal finance.

Why I want this?

By increasing my financial literacy, I can make informed financial decisions, understand financial jargon, and improve my overall financial well-being.
What's the impact of not doing anything about this?
Without financial literacy, I may struggle to understand financial concepts, make poor financial decisions, and miss out on potential opportunities.

6. Set up an emergency fund to prepare for unexpected expenses.

Why I want this?
By setting up an emergency fund, I can have peace of mind knowing that I'm financially prepared for unexpected expenses such as medical bills or car repairs.

What's the impact of not doing anything about this?
Without an emergency fund, unexpected expenses can cause financial stress, debt, and potentially harm my credit score.

Your career:

1. Obtain a new certification or degree to increase job prospects and earning potential.

Why I want this?
Obtaining a new certification or degree can open up new career opportunities and increase earning potential.

What's the impact of not doing anything about this?

Not obtaining new certifications or degrees can limit career advancement and earning potential, and may result in fewer job opportunities.

2. Develop new skills in a specific area of expertise to enhance job performance.

Why I want this?
Developing new skills can lead to greater job satisfaction and performance, and can make one more competitive in the job market.

What's the impact of not doing anything about this?
Not developing new skills may result in a lack of growth and development in one's career, and may limit opportunities for advancement.

3. Attend networking events and conferences to expand professional connections.

Why I want this?
Attending networking events and conferences can lead to new professional connections and potential job opportunities.

What's the impact of not doing anything about this?
Not attending networking events and conferences may result in missed opportunities for career advancement and professional growth

.

4. Create a five-year career plan with specific goals and action steps.

Why I want this?
Creating a career plan can help to set specific goals and create a roadmap for career advancement and success.

What's the impact of not doing anything about this?
Not having a career plan can result in a lack of direction and focus in one's career, and may lead to missed opportunities for growth and advancement.

5. Seek mentorship or coaching from a successful profession-al in your field.

Why I want this?
Seeking mentorship or coaching can provide valuable guidance and support for career development and growth.

What's the impact of not doing anything about this?
Not seeking mentorship or coaching may result in missed opportunities for learning and development, and may limit opportunities for career advancement.

6. Improve time management and productivity to increase efficiency at work.

Why I want this?
Improving time management and productivity can lead to increased efficiency and effectiveness in one's work, and can lead to greater career success.

What's the impact of not doing anything about this?
Not improving time management and productivity may result in missed deadlines and decreased job performance, which can negatively impact career success and advancement.

Your love life:

1. Prioritize quality time with your partner to strengthen the relationship.

Why I want this?
To maintain a strong connection with my partner and improve the quality of the relationship.

What's the impact of not doing anything about this?
Neglecting quality time with my partner may lead to a weaker connection and a less fulfilling relationship.

2. Practice active listening and effective communication to better understand each other's needs and concerns.

Why I want this?
To improve communication and understanding within the relationship, leading to stronger trust and connection.

What's the impact of not doing anything about this?
Poor communication and a lack of understanding can lead to misunderstandings, disagreements, and a weakened relationship.

3. Show appreciation and affection through small gestures like surprise dates or thoughtful gifts.

Why I want this?
To express love and affection towards my partner and maintain a strong emotional connection.

What's the impact of not doing anything about this?
A lack of appreciation and affection may lead to feelings of neglect or unimportance in the relationship.

4. Practice forgiveness and work through conflicts in a healthy and constructive way.

Why I want this?
To maintain a healthy and strong relationship by resolving conflicts and moving past disagreements.

What's the impact of not doing anything about this?
Holding onto resentment and not resolving conflicts can lead to further issues in the relationship and a weaker bond.

5. *Explore new activities and interests together to deepen the bond.*

Why I want this?
To strengthen the connection with my partner and create new shared experiences and memories.

What's the impact of not doing anything about this?
A lack of shared experiences and interests may lead to a less fulfilling relationship and a weakened connection.

6. *Continuously work on personal growth and self-improvement to be the best partner you can be.*

Why I want this?
To improve myself and the relationship with my partner by being the best version of myself.

What's the impact of not doing anything about this?
Neglecting personal growth and self-improvement may lead to stagnation in the relationship and a weaker bond.

Setting a compelling life vision is essential for achieving success and fulfilment in life. It provides a clear direction, a sense of purpose, and a motivation to pursue your goals. As I close my eyes and perform a guided meditation or visualization, I see myself in five years' time, living a life that is aligned with my vision.

In my vision, I see myself living a life that is full of meaning, purpose, and joy. I am in a career that I am passionate about and that allows me to make a positive impact on the world. I have financial stability and am able to provide for myself and my loved ones. My relationships with family and friends are strong and supportive. I am healthy, physically fit, and mentally balanced. I am constantly learning and growing, and am able to use my knowledge and skills to contribute to the world in a meaningful way.

With this compelling vision in mind, I am motivated to act towards achieving my goals. I am willing to make sacrifices, work hard, and stay committed to my vision. This mental state, attitude, and behaviour will ultimately alter my entire life, helping me to achieve my dreams and live a life of purpose and fulfilment. The seed is now planted, and I am excited to see what the future holds.

BRINGING IT ALL TOGETHER:
Part B - Now We Get SMART

As you transition from designing your life to planning your life, you realize that cheating your life vision into existence is not possible. Achieving your goals requires careful planning and intentional effort. Your mind is competent enough to achieve the life vision you are creating, but you must be diligent in your goal-setting approach.

Goal-setting is a learned skill that is essential for success in any aspect of life. The quote by Abraham Lincoln, "A goal properly set is half way achieved," emphasizes the importance of setting clear and specific goals. When you set a goal, you must be clear about what you want to achieve and develop a plan of action to get there. Here, your plan must be specific, measurable, achievable, relevant, and time-bound (SMART).

The quote by Brian Tracy, "An average person with clear goals will outperform a genius who doesn't know what he wants every single day of the week," highlights the importance of having clear goals. You must be specific and intentional about what you want to accomplish. A clear goal provides focus and direction, which is essential in achieving success.

Planning your life involves setting short-term and long-term goals. Short-term goals are the stepping stones to achieving long-term goals. These goals are typically achievable within a few months to a year. Long-term goals, on the other hand, require more time and effort to achieve, typically several years or even a lifetime. When setting goals, it is important to ensure that they align with your life vision and values.

In fact, studies have shown that an average person with clear goals will outperform a genius who doesn't know what they want. This is because having clear goals helps to guide your actions and decisions, making it easier to stay focused and motivated.

The process of setting goals involves identifying what you want to achieve, breaking it down into smaller, achievable steps, and developing a plan of action to get there. It is important to be realistic about the resources you have available, including time, money, and support, and to prioritize your goals based on their importance. Additionally, it is important to regularly review and adjust your goals as necessary to ensure that you are on track to achieving your life vision.

Remember, transitioning from designing your life to planning your life requires you to set clear goals that align with your life vision. You cannot cheat your way to your desired future. But with a competent mind and a clear plan of action, you can achieve the life vision that you're in the process of creating right now. So start setting your goals today and work towards the life you want to live.

So, now our goals will have to be SMART:

- Specific – can be easily described to another person

- Measurable – quantifiable

- Attainable – within realms of what I can achieve because if the bar is too high its going to drain my energy

- Relevant (rewarding) – set the bar high enough for it to fuel me and teach me

- Time Bound – deadlines make the goals real

As you continue your journey of goal-setting, it's important to keep in mind that time and resources are limited. Therefore, it's crucial to identify the highest leverage points and prioritize those goals. One tool that can be helpful in identifying these high leverage points is the Pareto 80/20 Principle.

The Pareto Principle, also known as the 80/20 rule, suggests that 80% of outcomes come from 20% of inputs. This principle can be applied to goal-setting by recognizing that 80% of your results will come from 20% of your efforts. Therefore, it's important to identify the most impactful goals and focus on those.

To identify the highest leverage goals, take a look at all your goals and select the goals that will have the greatest impact on your life vision. Start by identifying the highest leverage goals within the the short-term. These goals should be achievable within a relatively short period and should provide momentum towards achieving your long-term goals.

First, let's focus on the short-term goals. Within the next 1 month, you may want to prioritize goals that require immediate action and have a high impact on your life. For example, you may want to focus on completing a project at work, improving your health through exercise or eating healthier, or learning a new skill that can benefit your career or personal life.

Within the next 3 months, you can start working on goals that require a bit more time and effort. These goals should still be high-impact and aligned with your overall life vision. Examples may include saving a certain amount of money, launching a new project or business idea, or taking a course to develop a new skill.

Within the next 6 months, you can start thinking about goals that require more planning and resources. These goals may include traveling to a new destination, starting a new hobby or passion project, or taking steps towards a major career change.

Moving on to the mid-term goals, you can focus on goals that can be achieved within 1-3 years. These goals should be aligned with your overall life vision and help you make progress towards your long-term goals. Examples may include paying off debt, advancing in your career or education, starting a family, or buying a new home.

Within 3-5 years, you can focus on more ambitious goals that require more planning, resources, and time. These goals may include starting a new business or venture, pursuing a major career change, or traveling to a dream destination.

Within 5-10 years, you can focus on goals that require long-term planning and vision. These goals may include achieving financial independence, reaching a certain level of career success, buying a second home, or starting a non-profit organization.

It is important to note that the above timeframes are not set in stone and can be adjusted based on your own personal circumstances and goals. It is also important to regularly review and adjust your goals as needed to ensure that they remain aligned with your life vision and priorities.

In conclusion, identifying the highest leverage points among your goals can help you focus your time and resources on what truly matters. By applying the Pareto 80/20 principle and prioritizing your goals within various timeframes, you can make progress towards achieving your life vision and creating the life you truly desire.

CONCLUSION

As you reflect on your life and consider your future, you realize the importance of setting goals. Without goals, you may drift aimlessly through life, never truly fulfilling your potential or achieving the life you envision for yourself. By setting goals, you can take control of your life, exercise agency over your choices, and consciously create the future you desire.

Why do you set goals? You set goals because you have a deep need to exercise control over your life. You want to be in charge of your own destiny and have a say in how your life unfolds. As Dane Rudhyar said, "Man can only become what he is able to consciously imagine." By visualizing your future and setting goals, you take the first step toward turning your dreams into reality.

Every great accomplishment was first imagined in the mind. From the invention of the lightbulb to the landing on the moon, every great achievement began with an idea. By setting goals and visualizing your future, you can turn your own ideas into reality. As Geddy Lee said, "If you decide not to decide, you still have made a choice." Every decision, whether conscious or not, shapes your life. By actively choosing your path through goal-setting, you take control of your destiny.

But setting goals is not enough. You must also take conscious, purposeful daily actions toward your life vision. As Napoleon Bonaparte said, "Take time to deliberate but when the time arrives stop thinking and go in." Knowing what you want is not enough; you must also act to make it a reality. By acting toward your goals, you make progress toward the life you envision for yourself.

As you consider your goals and envision your future, it is important to become aware of any gaps between your daily actions and your desired outcomes. Does the reality of your daily actions match your daily rhetoric? If there is a gap between what you preach and what you practice, you must take steps to align your actions with your goals. You must ensure that your daily choices and actions are consistent with your life vision. As Johann Von Goethe said, "Knowing is not enough, we must apply."

To get crystal clear on your life vision, you must define with absolute clarity the person you want to become and the life you want to live. You must ask yourself, "What do I believe about this category? What exactly do I want in this category? Why do I want that? What exactly do I need to do to get it?" By answering these questions, you can gain a deeper understanding of your goals and what you need to do to achieve them.

As you work toward your goals, you will stretch and expand your field of awareness. You will become more conscious of the beliefs and actions that control your success in each area of your life. You will discover things you want in each area and examine the purpose of your desires. By taking deliberate, purposeful actions toward your life vision, you will become the person you want to be and live the life you want to live.

In conclusion, setting goals is essential for taking control of your life and creating the future you desire. By setting goals and acting toward them, you exercise agency over your choices and consciously create the future you want. To get crystal clear on your life vision, you must define with absolute clarity the person you want to become and the life you want to live. By taking conscious, purposeful daily actions toward your life vision, you can achieve success in all areas of your life.